Timmis and de la Hoyde remind us  book of the inestimable blessin~ ok is theologically rich but al. r. *In Christ* isn't merely unpac lied to our lives, so that we are ....ıst.

...mas R. Schreiner
James Buchanan Harrison Pr.... ut New Testament Interpretation
The Southern Baptist Theological Seminary
Louisville, KY

The New Testament *rarely* calls believers 'Christians'; we modern believers almost never call ourselves anything else. The New Testament *regularly* describes believers as those who are 'in Christ'; modern believers almost never do. The result? A widespread loss of the sheer grandeur of what it means to belong to Jesus Christ.

Thankfully, Steve Timmis and Christopher de la Hoyde 'get it'. The infectious enthusiasm, pastoral sensitivity, and enviable clarity with which this book has been written will help you to 'get it' too. If you do not *daily* think of yourself as someone who is 'in Christ' you simply *MUST* read this book.

Sinclair B. Ferguson
Associate Preacher
St Peter's Free Church
Dundee

Do not be deceived by this book's size or weight! Steve Timmis and Christopher de la Hoyde have written something weighty and rich that will be of huge benefit. Guided through crucial biblical chapters by great divines of the past like John Calvin and John Murray, we are given wonderful highlights of this tragically neglected doctrine. What treasure it is to be reminded that in Christ, we truly can have 'the full assurance of faith'. This is a book, and a doctrine, to return to frequently.

Mark Meynell
Associate Director – Europe (Langham Partnership), London

This is a splendid book, ideal for all Christians. Steve Timmis and Christopher de la Hoyde explain this vital and central truth of the gospel clearly and readably, and relate it to a range of real and practical situations which we all face. It deserves a wide readership.

Robert Letham
Director of Research and Senior Lecturer in Systematic and Historical Theology, Wales Evangelical School of Theology

I have long been an admirer of Steve Timmis, his writings and the wonderful contribution he is to the kingdom of God. This book, *In Christ*, not only deepens that admiration, but intensifies my affections for Christ. As the title suggests, *In Christ*, is a thoroughly Christo-centric volume, reminding the believer that everything we are and hope to be is rooted in the person of Christ, and brought about by His precious Holy Spirit.

Bryan Loritts
Author, *Letters to a Birmingham Jail*
Lead Pastor, Fellowship Memphis
Memphis, Tennessee

The profound truth of our union with Christ is deftly explained in this book. And the ways in which this truth affects the lives of believers, the church, and mission is helpfully laid forth. All believers will benefit from reflecting deeply on its message.

Constantine R. Campbell
Associate Professor of New Testament
Trinity Evangelical Divinity School
Deerfield, Illinois

In Christ

In Him together for the World

STEVE TIMMIS

AND

CHRISTOPHER DE LA HOYDE

Porterbrook
NETWORK

CHRISTIAN
FOCUS

Steve Timmis lives in Sheffield where he is a pastor in The Crowded House. He is the Executive Director of the Acts 29 Network. He is married to Janet and they have four married children, and currently eight grandchildren.

Christopher de la Hoyde grew up in Yorkshire and became a Christian while at university in Cambridge. He and his wife are part of Acts 29 Europe and lead Grace Church in Boroughbridge, North Yorkshire.

Copyright © Steve Timmis and Christopher de la Hoyde 2014
paperback ISBN 978-1-78191-429-8
epub ISBN 978-1-78191-509-7
Mobi ISBN 978-1-78191-513-4

10 9 8 7 6 5 4 3 2 1

Published in 2014
by
Christian Focus Publications Ltd,
Geanies House, Fearn,
Ross-shire, IV20 1TW, Scotland.
www.christianfocus.com
and
Porterbrook Network
215 Sharrow Vale Road
Sheffield, S11 8ZB
www.porterbrooknetwork.org

Cover design
by
Daniel van Straaten

Printed by
Bell and Bain, Glasgow

CONTENTS

Introduction

It was the week our little team was being sent out from mother church to plant a new church focused on a particular part of the city. To that end, we were meeting with some more experienced church-planters to get their advice, and the first question was this: 'What is the key thing a church-planter needs to know and teach a new church plant?'

I wonder how you would have answered that question. Maybe you would have said it was an understanding of the church: what the church is, what it's for, how it functions. You might have said that a robust understanding of *ecclesiology* was the key to seeing a new church thrive. Maybe, on the other hand, you would have pointed to mission: if the church exists *for* mission and *through* mission, then surely helping those engaged in a new church-plant to

develop a strong *missiology* must be essential in helping
that church live out its identity. Maybe you would have
said that *pneumatology* was the key – learning to rely on
and to follow the leading of the Spirit in everything; or
even *eschatology* – helping the church to keep its eyes on
the ultimate goal in all things: the establishment of a new
heavens and a new earth at the appearing of Christ.

But here's the question: what would John Calvin, the
great French Reformer, have said, if he'd been in the room?
I suspect that, after first saying, 'Pardon, je ne comprends
pas l'anglais' (and having asked for an interpreter), he
would have said: 'That's simple: teach them about what
it means to be united with Christ.' Here is what Calvin
writes about union with Christ in his *Institutes*:

> We see that our whole salvation and all its parts are
> comprehended in Christ ... This union (with Christ)
> alone ensures that, as far as we are concerned, he has not
> unprofitably come with the name of Saviour.[1]

For Calvin, this was the doctrine from which all other
doctrine – and all Christian living – flowed. John Owen
regarded it with equal magnitude:

> This is the cause of all other graces that we are made
> partakers of; they are all communicated unto us by
> virtue of our union with Christ. Hence is our adoption,
> our justification, our sanctification, our fruitfulness, our
> perseverance, our resurrection, our glory.[2]

---

1   John Calvin, *Institutes of the Christian Religion*, 2.16.19 & 3.1.3.

2   John Owen, *An Exposition of the Epistle to the Hebrews*, 21:149-50 (as
     quoted in J. V. Fesko, *John Owen on Union with Christ and Justification*,
     http://thegospelcoalition.org/themelios/article/john_owen_on_union_
     with_christ_and_justification/#, footnote 24).

John Murray likewise called it 'the central truth of the whole doctrine of salvation'.[3]

If these three 'weighty' theologians are right and the doctrine of union with Christ is the central tenet of the Christian faith – the spring from which all else flows – then everything we believe and do depends on the fact and nature of the relationship that exists between Jesus Christ and believers. A profound understanding of our union with Christ is critical for all church leadership and church-planting.

We sometimes hear the gospel being explained to children something like this: 'When you believe in Jesus and trust him for your sins, Jesus lives in your heart.' It is tempting to be critical of the simplicity of that explanation. It sounds a bit 'twee'. Wise adults see theological truths missed out, and might feel sceptical about the summing up of salvation as 'Jesus lives in your heart'. But the truth is that that simple line articulates something profound about the wonder and mystery of the gospel. Jesus *does* live in us. And we live in Him. It is a miracle of supernatural grace; a breathtaking condescension; an all-powerful love that unites us intimately with Christ Jesus. And because of that union, all of the riches of heaven are ours. John Calvin defined union with Christ as 'the union by which we grow together with him so that he revives us by his Spirit and transfers his power to us.'[4]

Union with Christ is truly phenomenal and supernatural, but it is not make-believe or mysterious. It is beautifully pertinent to daily experience. As the central doctrine of the Christian faith it incorporates and expresses all that

---

3   John Murray, *Redemption Accomplished and Applied* (W. B. Eerdmans, 1955), p. 161.

4   John Calvin, *Commentaries*, Volume XXXVIII, Romans ch. 6, v. 5.

God has planned from eternity past, through time, and into eternity future.

The aim of this book is to show how our union with Christ really does shape and impact not only everything we do and say, but how we say and do it. It defines our theology in all of its aspects: soteriology, pneumatology, eschatology, missiology. But it also defines and shapes how we live.

It reverberates out into our pursuit of godliness. The more we understand the nature of who we are in Christ, the less we will sin. We sin because, in that moment, we forget who we are in Christ. We pretend to be something we are no longer. We are masquerading as 'in Adam', when the truth for Christians is that we are 'in Christ'.

It reverberates in our shared life in community, because union with Christ necessarily involves union with all those who are also united with Christ. In His so-called 'High Priestly prayer', Jesus prays for unity among His people: 'The glory that you have given me I have given to them, that they may be one even as we are one, I in them and you in me, that they may become perfectly one...' (John 17:22-23).

It reverberates in our witness to the world in mission because as we realise the utter futility of seeking to accomplish anything apart from Christ, we also know the security and joy of our identity in Him. Our union with Christ is the single best motivation for faithfulness and perseverance in proclaiming the gospel and in living for Christ before a watching world.

One

Safe
in Christ

Imagine a painting of a house. The house is engulfed by threatening storm clouds and lightning, and is being buffeted by the weather. One brilliant white flash of lightning strikes a large tree in the background, the surrounding scenery is blown about by the wind and there are lashes of rain hitting the sides of the house. But in the midst of that dangerous storm, the sturdy house is a secure and peaceful place. It is a haven in the storm. The lights are on inside, and they shine golden through the windows.

This scene of storm and threat is a biblical image of judgement. The house represents Christ. The gospel invites us into that house, so that we might be hidden from the storm of God's judgement. In that house we find peace and safety – absolute protection from the deadly storm outside.

That is the gospel invitation: come into Christ, escape from judgement and enjoy great blessing. Outside is the threat of deluge, of being struck by lightning or blown away by a typhoon. Every conceivable image of danger is outside of the house. But *in* that house, you are secure. Nothing is going to break through the shelter of that house. Inside, there is blessing. There is food, warmth, comfort. Everything is to be enjoyed there, inside the house.

This is a simple depiction of the *locational* view of union with Christ. Over the next two chapters we will look at four important aspects of what union with Christ means: location, representation, relationship and presence with God. In doing so, we will see two things. First, we will see that union with Christ is not simply a New Testament idea: rather, it is a great truth which echoes and fulfils themes that have been running all the way through the Bible. Second, we will see that our union with Christ in the Spirit is the foundation of all our security and blessing in the gospel.

LOCATION

Eden

Genesis 2 tells the story of creation. On two occasions the narrator shows God placing man in a garden. The first one is in verse 8: 'Now the LORD God had planted a garden in the east, in Eden; and there he put the man he had formed.' The second is verse 15: 'The LORD God took the man and put him in the Garden of Eden to work it and take care of it.' The repetition here is striking, because the second one follows the first so closely: 'and there he put the man'; 'God took the man and put him in the garden'.

Two things in particular are worthy of note. First, the Lord's deliberate, purposeful action. Man didn't simply *end up* in the garden. He didn't stumble upon it as he was looking for a place to call his own. The Lord planted a garden, and then put man there. It is quite clear that the garden was planted for Adam. It was to be humanity's home.

Second, it was *a garden*. The word depicts an enclosed area that conjures up images of a park, surrounded by a hedge. The Lord had made the universe vast and complex. In that unfathomable expanse, He placed Planet Earth. And on that planet, with a surface area of over 510,000,000 sq. km, the Lord planted a garden where He placed the first man.

It is helpful to note, as G.K. Beale points out, that garden imagery in the Ancient Near East represented temples and royalty.[1] In Genesis we see God's very presence there in Eden – God the King, presiding in His temple-house. In that place there is security and blessing for Adam and Eve. Beale says that 'the Garden of Eden was the first archetypal temple in which the first man worshipped God.'[2]

That garden is described in a striking way in verse 9: 'The Lord God made all kinds of trees grow out of the ground – trees that were pleasing to the eye and good for food.' It is a place of abundance and provision. Man could live there and want for nothing. It wasn't too long before the man was joined in this place of grace by God's kindest

---

1   Beale's *The Temple and the Church's Mission: A Biblical Theology of the Dwelling Place of God* (New Studies in Biblical Theology 17, Apollos/IVP, 2004) is an excellent resource for further exploring these themes.

2   Ibid., p. 66.

gift to him, Eve. French theologian Henri Blocher makes the point that 'we are to understand that no riches of any sort are lacking in Eden'.[3] Everything was as it should be there in the garden.

When sin came in, however (Genesis 3), and God visited Adam and Eve in grace and judgement, He expelled them from the garden, on the east side (3:24).

The Land of Promise

In Genesis 11, we read the curious story of Babel. The restless human race finds an expansive plain, settles there and holds the first global conference. Two points are worth mentioning from this passage. First, the decision to settle was in direct contradiction of the command to 'fill the earth'. Second, the migration is said to be 'eastward' (v. 2).

So far in Genesis, 'east' has proved to be a significant marker, cf. 2:8; 3:24; 4:16; 10:30. The writer is not primarily interested in geographical detail or in historical accuracy (though neither of these is irrelevant). Rather, the scene is being set for a significant reversal.

Once more, as in 3:8, at the very point of sin, the Lord comes to His people in both grace and judgement. Then, out of this migrating mass of humanity, He calls Abraham out of Ur, in the general vicinity of Babel, and makes some remarkable promises. Integral to those promises is a land:

> Now the LORD said to Abram, 'Go from your country and your kindred and your father's house to the land that I will show you. And I will make of you a great nation, and I will bless you and make your name great, so that you will be a blessing. I will bless those who bless you,

---

3   Henri Blocher, *In the Beginning* (InterVarsity Press, 1984), p. 114.

and him who dishonours you I will curse, and in you all
the families of the earth shall be blessed.' (Gen. 12:1-3)

The Lord led Abraham and brought him into Canaan.
There, the Lord promised that Abraham's children and
descendants would inherit that land (v. 7). The story of
Abraham, from that point onwards, is about him learning
to trust in God and the promises the Lord makes. But
these promises are neither other-worldly nor insubstantial.
They concern a specific, locatable piece of real estate. It
was in that land that Abraham and his descendants would
be blessed.

As we have seen, in Eden the man and woman had
everything for the taking – fruit which they could simply
pluck (Gen. 1:29-30). But after the perplexing act of
disobedience, the Lord cursed the earth so that it yielded
its fruit reluctantly. Man could still eat of it, but he would
now be able only to eke out an existence: it would be
harvested only through thorns and thistles, and by blood,
sweat and tears.

The land the Lord promised Abraham, however, was
different. It is described as 'a land flowing with milk and
honey' (Deut. 11:9). In that land, God promised Abraham's
descendants to bless the fruit of their womb, their crops,
their wine, their oil and their livestock (Deut. 7:13).
Everything the people considered rich and sumptuous
would be there for the taking. It seemed too good to be
true. It was as if God was saying, 'You know the land of
Eden, where I placed your relatives – the land I'm giving
you now is like that.' It was as though it would be a place
that didn't know God's curse.

This is why He did not lead His people out of Egypt
to Mount Sinai and then tell them to wander around the

wilderness for a while and decide where they wanted to live. There was only one place that was ordained for them: it was in the land that they would be blessed.

Judgement

Psalm 37:3 says this: 'Trust in the Lord and do good; dwell in the land and enjoy safe pasture' (NIV). The context of the people of Israel was an agrarian one; their herds were a means of wealth and production. The idea that you could leave your flock to graze in safety was a glorious mark of God's blessing. There 'in the land' is the location of God's blessing.

But when the Lord judged Israel because of their faithlessness, He raised up enemies against them and through them provided warnings and tasters that the land would be the focus of His judgement as well as His grace. The land was the means by which God mediated His blessings on His people, but 'in the land' was also the place where He mediated His judgement. Exclusion from the land was God's ultimate judgement: 'How can we sing the Lord's song in a strange land?', the people lament in Psalm 137. Being in exile, outside of the land, destroyed the very sense of identity of the people of God.

The Old Testament ends on a negative note. The people of Israel are back in the land: God's promises of a return to Canaan have proved true. Yet things aren't as they should be because the people are still rebelling, as the final chapters of Nehemiah show vividly. Nehemiah desperately tries to cleanse the people of their Sabbath-breaking and inter-marriage with the idolatrous Moabites. And yet we sense that this will be a fruitless effort. God's people are not loving God well and faithfully. There are 400 years of silence – and then Matthew's Gospel opens.

Christ Jesus

Everything we read about in Matthew takes place 'in the land', the same land promised to Abraham thousands of years earlier. Equally significant is that all that God had promised to Abraham and his progeny occurs 'in the land'. The birth of the Messiah is 'in the land'. In the third and fourth chapters of Matthew, Jesus' baptism and temptation are 'in the land'. Baptism by John in the River Jordan conjures up memories of the route by which the people of Israel entered the land in the first place. In a sense, with Jesus as the true Son of God, this was a homecoming, a return from exile, a new beginning. Jesus begins His ministry 'in the land', and it becomes once again a land of blessing. The dead are raised. The hungry are fed. The sick are healed. Sins are forgiven. The land was now, at last, the place it was meant to be.

But then something almost inexplicable happens. After Acts 8, with the persecution of Stephen, the church is scattered. And now this land, which is so prominent all the way through the Old Testament and even through the four Gospels, disappears from view. We do not find any more references to being 'in the land'. Suddenly, something significant becomes simply insignificant! Why is this?

It has been replaced by that to which it pointed – Jesus. Being 'in Christ' is the refrain echoing through the pages of the New Testament. Being 'in the land' was just a hint – an indication, a promise – of God's ultimate blessing which comes to us in Christ. So in Ephesians 1:3 we read that 'we are blessed with every spiritual blessing in the heavenly places, in Christ Jesus.'

Going back to our first illustration, that house is a place of blessing. Everything your heart desires is there, 'in

Christ'. The gospel call is saying those two things: come
into Christ where you will have blessing; come into Christ
and therefore escape from judgement. G. K. Beale points
out that Christ is now the temple – the same dwelling-
place of God which is imaged in Eden. This temple, and
therefore locational, imagery stretches throughout the
whole of the biblical narrative:

> The Edenic imagery describing the city-temple in
> Revelation 22:1-3 also reflects an intention to show that
> the building of the temple that began in Genesis 2 but
> was abandoned, will be commenced again and completed
> in Christ and his people, and will encompass the whole
> new creation.[4]

Not only was Jesus born in the land, and not only did He live
and minister in the land, He also died there. In His death
He was cut off from the land: exiled, as it were. The exile to
Babylon of up to 40,000 Jews in 586 B.C. was just a foretaste
and precursor of this ultimate exile. Jesus was outside of the city,
He was cut off from the people. He was the ultimate reject. As
He was lifted up on the cross, earth rejected Him and the doors
of heaven were closed to Him. In those hours of darkness,
stranded and skewered, when even His Father turned His face
from Him, He became the ultimate cursed one.

He endured judgement, and we died with Him. As
those 'in Christ' – united with Him by His Spirit, through
faith – when He died, we died. Just as there is blessing
'in Christ', so too Christ is the one who mediates God's
judgement. Because we are 'in Him', we are secure. Jesus
took the judgement in Himself; He bore the judgement
instead of us. We are safe 'in Him'. We no longer have to

---

4   G. K. Beale, *The Temple and the Church's Mission*, p. 170.

fear God's judgement. God the Father turned His face in anger from His Son 2,000 years ago at Calvary. Because of this the Father will never turn His face from us in anger nor reject us for our sin.

That is the glory of what it is to be in Christ. This is a very rich biblical theme. Whenever you read about the land in the Old Testament, remember that it is there to point you to what it means to be 'in Christ' in the gospel. Whatever blessings the Israelites enjoyed in the land are nothing compared to the blessings we enjoy 'in Christ'.[5]

REPRESENTATION

Representation is a difficult concept for those of us living in a western context to grasp. We understand individual responsibility, partly because we are so immersed in a culture of individualism. We are committed to individualism. We can accept that if we personally do something wrong, we should suffer for it. But the thought that we should suffer for what someone else did, or that someone else should suffer for us, is an alien idea.

Think of the Olympic Games, however. The concept of representation is very clear in that sporting event. The athletes do not compete simply as individuals, running, swimming, fighting, jumping, riding, throwing or leaping for their own glory. When we talk about the Olympics with our friends, we commonly use language such as: 'We won three medals last night', or, 'It was sad that we lost out on that gold – but we won silver for the first time in forty years.' If we know someone from another country,

---

5 For a detailed look at these themes we highly recommend chapters 5 and 6 of Beale's *The Temple and the Church's Mission*. Pages 216-45 are particularly instructive on this topic.

we ask, 'How many medals have you won?' It is clear that we, as individuals, have not won any medals. And yet, we have! The athletes are our representatives. We feel a surge of patriotism because of what they have accomplished.

Representation in Romans

Understanding representation is key to understanding our union with Christ. Jesus represents us. He stands for us: His death is our death and His life is our life. Romans 3:21-24 is profound and wonderful:

> But now the righteousness of God has been manifested apart from the law, although the Law and the Prophets bear witness to it—the righteousness of God through faith in Jesus Christ for all who believe. For there is no distinction: for all have sinned and fall short of the glory of God, and are justified by his grace as a gift, through the redemption that is in Christ Jesus.

In Romans 3:20 Paul asserts that there is none righteous, not one. All the world is laid level in its sin and need. But in Christ, God gave Himself, and He achieved salvation for us. God's answer to the human predicament, in sin and under judgement, is Christ. There is redemption only 'in Christ'.

Paul goes on to discuss Abraham, showing that it is faith in the promises of God that made Abraham righteous (4:3). And then Paul says that that is exactly the way it is with us:

> But the words 'it was counted to him' were not written for his sake alone, but for ours also. It will be counted to us who believe in him who raised from the dead Jesus our Lord, who was delivered up for our trespasses and raised for our justification (4:23-24).

Jesus was there as our substitute. It is through faith, trust and confidence in what God has done in Christ that we are made right with God. 'Therefore,' Paul says in chapter 5, 'since we have been justified by faith, we have peace with God through our Lord Jesus Christ. Through him we have also obtained access by faith into this grace in which we stand' (vv. 1-2). So as we go into this house, which is Christ, we stand in Him – we stand in grace so that judgement will never touch us.

In the second half of chapter 5, Paul then points us to Adam, our first representative: '...sin came into the world through one man, and death through sin, and so death spread to all men because all sinned' (v. 12). Of course, we know that we all sin. This is the story of the Bible. In Genesis 3, Adam sins. In Genesis 4, Cain repeats that sin, and from then on sin spreads. In Romans chapter 3 Paul has pointed out our individual guilt for personal sin. But that is not what Paul is saying here. Here, Paul is talking about representation. He is saying that when Adam sinned, as our representative, we all sinned. When Adam sinned it wasn't just his future that was being determined, but the future of all humanity. The whole of humanity were there 'in Adam', as our representative head. His failure is our problem. Our sin, the individual sin that we commit, is because in Adam we sinned. The sin that we commit is a consequence of the sin that Adam committed. It isn't simply that we repeat Adam's sin, though we do do that. Rather, he set the tone for all human experience. Because of Adam we are born into an environment in which sin is the norm. Adam's sin is our sin; and Adam's condemnation is our condemnation.

Paul's principal point, however, is that Adam's failure is not the end of the story. In fact, it is just the beginning. 'But the free gift is not like the trespass. For if many died through one man's trespass, much more have the grace of God and the free gift by the grace of that one man Jesus Christ abounded for many!' (5:15). If Adam as our representative is bad news, Jesus Christ as our representative is glorious.

Paul sees only these two categories: we are either 'in Adam' or we are 'in Christ'. The gospel is God's command and invitation for us to come out of Adam: out of sin and judgement. The gospel is also God's command and invitation for us to come into Christ. The good in Christ is so much better than the bad in Adam.

> For if, because of one man's trespass, death reigned through that one man, much more will those who receive the abundance of grace and the free gift of righteousness reign in life through the one man Jesus Christ. (5:17)

Paul delights to maximise Christ as the representative head. It is a sorry picture 'in Adam'; it is nothing but glorious 'in Christ'.

> Therefore, as one trespass led to condemnation for all men, so one act of righteousness leads to justification and life for all men. (5:18)

Paul is driving this point home: it is all about representation. So the question we have to ask is: am I in Adam, or am I in Christ? Who is my representative head? Upon whose work am I depending? To depend on Adam is foolish. The result of what he did was nothing but death, curse, suffering and misery. But if I am in Christ, then the result of what Christ achieved is nothing but this: glory, blessing, life, righteousness. Everything for which our hearts instinctively yearn is true in Christ.

Two

Connected in Christ

If location and representation were the only ways the Bible spoke about union with Christ we would be tempted to see it as a somewhat cold and impersonal doctrine. Old Testament believers enjoyed God's blessings *in the land*, yet they had no *personal relationship* with the land. Likewise, we may share in the victories of our nation's athletes because they represent us, but this does not lead us into a *personal relationship* with those athletes. To understand this intimately relational aspect of our union with Christ, we must turn to the work of the Spirit.

UNION WITH CHRIST ONLY IN THE SPIRIT

Union with Christ is possible only through the work of God the Spirit. Every aspect of salvation and the application of Christ's finished work is related to, and dependent on, the Spirit's work in uniting us to Christ.

The contribution made by each member of the Trinity to our salvation is distinct, but there is a sense in which we can only 'formally' distinguish the work of the Holy Spirit from the work of the Son and that of the Father. Functionally, the work of each one is inseparable from that of the other two and all their works are mutually interdependent. To delight in the miracle of grace that is ours in Christ we must acknowledge that 'secret energy of the Spirit'[1] which effects every saving change in our hearts, from conviction through conversion and all the way through to the new creation. The specific and particular work of the Spirit is the channel of every joy that is ours in Christ.

Romans chapter 8 has been described as the most comprehensive section in the Bible on the role of the Spirit in our salvation. It is not difficult to see why. In chapter 5, as we have seen, Paul has been demonstrating how believers are justified entirely and uniquely by faith in Christ, and how the grace of God in Christ super-abounds over sin and death: the issue is simply whether we are 'in Adam' or 'in Christ'.

In chapters 6 and 7, however, Paul answers two questions that might be elicited by such a bold statement of God's super-abounding grace in Christ: 'Are we to continue in sin that grace may abound?' (6:1) and, 'Is the law sin?' (7:7). Paul answers these questions in turn.

First, in 6:1-6 he shows that our union with Christ in His death and resurrection means that we cannot continue in sin: we died and were raised with Christ, and

---

1　　John Calvin, *Institutes*, 3.3.1.

so are to count ourselves 'dead to sin and alive to God in Christ Jesus' (6:11). We will return to this theme in the next chapter.

Second, in 7:7-8:4 he shows that the Law is not sin: it is both good (7:12) and effective (7:13), because it was given by God for the specific purpose of exposing sin and leading people to Christ (what he calls a 'schoolmaster' or 'guardian' in Galatians 3:24). It is true that the Law could never justify or sanctify, but that is because the Law was never given with those ends in view. The Law did what it was meant to do – nothing more and nothing less.

The contrast with the work of the Spirit in chapter 8, however, could not be more pronounced. Picking up his argument from 5:21[2], Paul asserts that 'there is now no condemnation for those who are in Christ Jesus'. Because Christ as our representative was condemned on the cross, condemnation is no longer a possibility or threat for us. Our union with Christ is so intimate that we shared His curse and now share His blessings. He paid the wages of sin and as a consequence we receive His life as a gift of God. All this is due to the Spirit, who, in uniting the believer to Christ, works powerfully to liberate us: 'For the law of the Spirit of life has set you free in Christ Jesus from the law of sin and death' (8:2). The Spirit has done what the Law could never do. How? By uniting us with Christ Jesus!

That is the key dimension of the Spirit's work: uniting the believer to Christ so that all of His achievements are ours. Calvin explains that it is through the Spirit that we obtain the benefits of salvation:

---

2   An alternative reading sees Paul picking up his argument from 7:6; cf. Thomas R. Schreiner, *Romans: Baker Exegetical Commentary on the New Testament* (Baker Academic, 1998), p. 398.

We must now examine this question. How do we receive those benefits which the Father bestowed on his only-begotten Son – not for Christ's own private use, but that he might enrich poor and needy men? First we must understand that as long as Christ remains outside of us, and we are separated from him, all that he has suffered and done for the salvation of the human race remains useless and of no value for us ... All that he possesses is nothing to us until we grow into one body with him. It is true that we obtain this by faith. Yet ... reason teaches us to climb higher and to examine into the secret energy of the Spirit, by which we come to enjoy Christ and all his benefits.[3]

Calvin's logic is irresistible: the Father gives believers His benefits only in Christ; believers are united with Christ by faith; and this faith comes exclusively from 'the secret energy of the Spirit' working within us. The Holy Spirit's work is therefore to bind us to Christ through faith.

An immediate, relational union

Calvin's understanding of salvation and how Christ and all His benefits are ours was in stark contrast to the general view that prevailed in the period leading up to the Reformation.

In the Middle Ages salvation was tied to the sacraments and God's grace was communicated to us in and through those rituals. Justification was a process which was mediated by the priests. As Sinclair Ferguson explains: 'the work of the Spirit was thus enclosed within the administration of the seven sacraments.' This sacramentalism saw the work of the Spirit as dependent upon the administration of the

---

3   John Calvin, *Institutes*, 3.1.1.

rituals of the Church.[4] As Ferguson notes, however: 'in the Reformation teaching it was emphasised that the Holy Spirit brought the individual directly into fellowship with Christ, of which fellowship the sacraments were seen as signs and seals.'[5]

It is part of the glory of the gospel that the work of the Spirit in uniting us to Christ is immediate and unmediated. There is *nothing* between the believer and Christ; no human, no ritual, no deed, no practice. The Father sends the Spirit, who takes us into the Son, and He does it all for His glory and our joy. Ferguson goes on to explain it in these terms:

> Every facet of the application of Christ's work ought to be related to the way in which the Spirit united us to Christ himself, and viewed as directly issuing from personal fellowship with him. The dominant motif principle of the order of salvation should therefore be union with Christ in the Spirit.[6]

Union with Christ *is* finding shelter from judgement in Jesus, just as we would step inside to get out of the rain. But it is also much more than that. The blessings of redemption come to us through actual participation in Christ. The work of the Holy Spirit makes union with Christ something active, organic and dynamic. It is a living relationship that secures for us all the blessings of salvation. We can sometimes unintentionally objectivise what happened on the cross by viewing the blessings of salvation as being won for us by Christ and then, at the

---

4   Sinclair B. Ferguson, *The Holy Spirit* (InterVarsity Press, 1997), pp. 94-5.

5   Ibid., p. 96.

6   Ibid., p. 100.

appropriate time, given to us. In point of fact, they are ours only in union with Christ through the Holy Spirit. Ferguson writes again:

> Calvin is underlining ... that the blessings of redemption ought not to be viewed as merely having Christ as their ultimate causal source but as being ours only by direct participation in Christ, in union with him through the Spirit.[7]

This union with Christ in the Spirit is therefore profoundly relational. Christ becomes our covenant partner, with the Holy Spirit binding us to Him, a union of which marriage is an analogy. In the profoundest sense possible, we are His, and He is ours. Because we are in Him, we are drawn into the intimate relationships of the Trinity: the Father loves us with the same love with which He loved the Son since before the foundation of the world (John 17:23-24); we are heirs of God and co-heirs with Christ (Rom. 8:17); Christ lives in us by *His Spirit*, 'the Spirit of Christ' (Rom. 8:9); and by the Spirit both the Son and the Father make their home in us (John 14:23).

We should not think, however, that this relational immediacy with the members of the Trinity because of our union with Christ is merely formal and objective, as if it were simply a set of truths to be pondered. Through the work of the Spirit, this union with Christ is intended by God to be an experiential reality for believers, because the Spirit helps us to enjoy the reality of our union with Christ. By the Spirit 'we cry, "Abba! Father!"' (Rom. 8:15). 'The Spirit himself bears witness with our spirit that we

---

7　　Ibid., p. 102.

are children of God' (Rom. 8:16). And Paul prays for the Ephesians that, 'according to the riches of his glory [the Father] may grant you to be strengthened with power through his Spirit in your inner being, so that Christ may dwell in your hearts through faith' (Eph. 3:16-17).

Our marriage union with Christ is not simply a theological truth: it is a real, intimate relationship with the lover of our soul, through which we enjoy sweet fellowship with all three members of the Trinity. Through our union with Christ in the Spirit we are to savour, revel in, delight in and commune with Christ Himself.

PRESENCE WITH GOD

One final aspect of our union with Christ deserves mention here. In Ephesians 2:4-6 Paul writes these incredible words:

> But God, being rich in mercy, because of the great love with which he loved us, even when we were dead in our trespasses, made us alive together with Christ—by grace you have been saved—and raised us up with him and seated us with him in the heavenly places in Christ Jesus.

It is an extraordinary statement: Paul says that, because we are united with Christ, we are *already* seated with Him in the heavenly places: not in the future, but *right now*. By virtue of our union with Christ, believers live their whole lives in the very presence of God.

What does he mean by this? Two things. First, Paul is highlighting the *access* that we have to God. Because we are in Christ, and Christ is with the Father, we – who were by nature children of wrath – have unfettered access to the throne-room of God: to the Father Himself. As the writer to the Hebrews puts it: 'Since we have a great high priest who has passed through the heavens, Jesus the Son of God, let us hold fast our confession ... Let us then with confidence draw near to the throne of grace, that we may receive mercy and find grace to help in time of need' (Heb. 4:14 and 16). In the Old Testament, the High Priest wore a breastplate with twelve jewels that represented the names of the twelve tribes of God's people (Exod. 28:15-21). Symbolically, the priest brought the people of God into the presence of God. This foreshadowed a day when God's real High Priest would stand in God's presence: not in a man-made tabernacle but in heaven itself; not just from time to time, but constantly; and not just symbolically bringing before God the names of the tribes of God's people, but actually bringing all those united with Him into the very presence of God. Because of our union with Christ, we are always in the presence of God, and have unlimited, unimpeded access to Him on His throne of grace.

Second, Paul is highlighting the absolute security that we have in Christ. If we are in Christ, and Christ is with God, then nothing can threaten our salvation. As Paul writes in Colossians: 'For you have died, and your life is hidden with Christ in God. When Christ who is your life appears, then you also will appear with Him in glory' (Col. 3:3-4). No spiritual forces can get in the way; no sin can cut us off from God; no disobedience can disqualify us; no unfinished obedience undo us. Why? Because our lives are hidden with Christ in the very presence of God until He returns: we are utterly safe in Him.

CONCLUSION
We will explore more fully the life-changing reverberations of our union with Christ in the following chapters. Having set out these four themes of location, representation,

relationship and the presence of God, however, there are two things we can conclude with certainty.

First, if we were not united to Christ, we would have no hope. Every blessing that the Father gives us, He gives us in His Son because the Father desires for His Son to be glorified in everything: '... all things were created through him and for him' (Col. 1:16). God's riches in Christ is the central theme of the Bible story; exploring, understanding and enjoying Christ and all the riches God has for us in Him are the central pursuits of the Christian life. As Calvin puts it: 'In short, since rich store of every kind of good abounds in him, let us drink our fill from this fountain, and from no other.'[8] For the church-planter or pastor, the key to seeing a Christian community flourish and bear fruit for the gospel is not strategy or clever missiology: it is growing in our knowledge of our union with Christ and helping those in our care to drink their fill 'from this fountain'.

Second, because of our union with Christ, we have absolute security with God. He will no more reject us than He will reject His Son whom He loves! Because we are united with the Son, all of His blessings are ours. Because we are united with the Son, everything He has achieved is credited to us. Because we are united to the Son, we have the same intimacy with the Father that Christ Himself has: He says of us: 'This is my son, whom I love: with him I am well pleased' (Matt. 3:17, NIV). Because we are united with the Son, we stand unmovable in God's presence until the Son returns. Our union with Christ is the source of all our confidence, all our hope and all our joy.

---

8   John Calvin, *Institutes*, 2.16.19.

Christ was given to us by God's generosity, to be grasped and possessed by us in faith. By partaking of him, we principally receive a double grace: namely, that being reconciled to God through Christ's blamelessness, we may have in heaven instead of a Judge a gracious Father; and secondly, that sanctified by Christ's Spirit we may cultivate blamelessness and purity of life.[1]

As we have seen, our union with Christ is a foundational element of gospel truth. It is foundational in two ways. First, everything else flows out from it: all of our blessings are the fruit of our union with Christ. Second, it is foundational in that it is the sure, steady rock upon which we build our Christian lives: our union with Christ is the unchangeable reality which guarantees our security with God. We must not, however, think of union with Christ as a static truth. Rather, it is a truth that transforms: it is dynamic.

Sanctification is a pressing and very personal issue for every one of us who is a Christian. We want to please Christ. We struggle with the fact of sin in our hearts and lives, and also with the very notion of sin. In moments of reflection, I know that sin is foolish, insane and utterly reprehensible. But I also know that in moments of temptation sin becomes utterly plausible. Somehow, that which was so vile becomes enticing, and sometimes irresistible to us. This is the conflicted existence with which we are all familiar. We can enjoy intimate and real fellowship with God, where our hearts are genuinely stirred and our affections warmed. But then, we get into the office and temptation strikes. All of that resolve and repulsion disappears, and sin becomes attractive.

---

1   John Calvin, *Institutes*, 3.11.1.

In his comments on 2 Timothy 3:16, Calvin wrote this: 'The right use of Scripture must always tend to what is profitable.'[2] Likewise, the right use of doctrine (which is all hewn from God's word) must always tend to what is profitable, because its purpose is to do us good. No truth is theoretical or academic; it is all practical and applied to 'equip us for every good work' (2 Tim. 3:17). So if we can see how the doctrine of union with Christ defines sanctification, we will be in a better position to understand the other blessings that are ours in Christ. And this will put us in a much better position to recognise the implications of the truth in our everyday struggle against sin.

WHAT IS SANCTIFICATION?

We will first define two elements of sanctification: *'progressive' sanctification* and *definitive sanctification*. Then we will look at Paul's understanding of sanctification in Romans 6, and the practical impact of this gospel truth in our daily lives.

'Progressive' sanctification

This is what most of us have in mind when we think about sanctification. Progressive sanctification is a term describing how a Christian grows in likeness to Jesus. It is about our desires, thoughts, ambitions and actions changing as we become more like Christ. John Murray describes this aspect of sanctification as:

> The process by which a believer is gradually transformed and conformed more and more into the image of Christ, until at death the disembodied spirit is made perfect in

---

2   John Calvin, *Commentaries*, Volume XLIII, 2 Timothy 3:16.

holiness and at the resurrection his body likewise will be conformed to the likeness of the body of Christ's glory.[3]

The word 'progressive', however, is not favoured by everyone. David Peterson says:

> Instead of speaking in terms of progressive sanctification, the New Testament more regularly employs the language of renewal, transformation and growth to describe what God is doing with us here and now.[4]

Peterson points out the danger of viewing this element of sanctification as a work that we do rather than God's gift. Holiness is both a gift and a calling; it has nothing to do with our efforts. So Peterson takes issue with the idea 'that there is a graded form of progress that can lead to ever increasing measures of holiness.'[5] This is because it creates unrealistic expectations which can lead to guilt and despair for those who don't see such 'progress' in their lives. Instead, 'pursue' is a helpful word to use in thinking about this process of growth and change. Those who have been won by Christ will want to pursue Christ, thus becoming more and more like Him in character. 'Those who have been sanctified through Christ will pursue the values and characteristics of the One to whom they belong.'[6] This transformative aspect of sanctification is important and valid. It is the work of God to make us ever more like His Son.

---

3   John Murray, 'Definitive Sanctification' in *Calvin Theological Journal*, 2:1 (April 1967), accessed via http://www.banneroftruth.org/pages/articles/article_print.php?1925 on 16th November 2012.

4   David Peterson, *Possessed by God: A New Testament Theology of Sanctification and Holiness* (Apollos/IVP, 1995, reprinted 2000), p. 136.

5   ibid., p.70.

6   ibid., p.76.

Definitive sanctification

Definitive sanctification says that in Christ we have been set apart by God, for God. It is a sovereign and decisive act of God. This understanding of sanctification is the more prevalent in the New Testament. At the point of conversion, believers are definitively, once-for-all sanctified or set apart for God. Sanctification is past-tense before it is progressive.

> We are thus compelled to take account of the fact that the language of sanctification is used with reference to some decisive action that occurs at the inception of the Christian life and one that characterises the people of God in their identity as called effectually by God's grace. It would be, therefore, a deflection from biblical patterns of language and conception to think of sanctification exclusively in terms of a progressive work.[7]

In the Old Testament we see that the sanctification of items and individuals was a central theme in Israel's Law. Everything to do with the tabernacle and temple was holy, e.g. garments (Exod. 28:2), anointing oil (Exod. 30:25), linen tunic (Lev. 16:4), feasts (Lev. 23:2), water (Num. 5:17), utensils (1 Kings 8:4). Vital to the building of both edifices was the 'sanctification' of craftsmen – trained and talented workers set apart for God to build a suitable venue for the Lord to meet with His people. The theologian Klaus Bockmuehl defines sanctification in the Old Testament as 'the act or process by which people or things are cleansed and dedicated to God, ritually and morally.'[8] This is the foundation for the doctrine of sanctification in the New Testament: in Christ we are set apart by God, for God.

---

7   John Murray, 'Definitive Sanctification'.

8   Klaus Bockmuehl, 'Sanctification', in S. B. Ferguson & D. F. Wright [eds], *New Dictionary of Theology* (Leicester/ Downers Grove: IVP, 1988), p. 613.

Our progressive, or transformative, sanctification is only possible because definitive sanctification has happened.

> Sanctification is a state in which believers find themselves because of the work of Christ and the operation of his Spirit in their lives. They are called to remain in that state 'by living in correspondence to their given holiness'. It is also a state to which they must strive, which they must 'pursue', or 'complete'.[9]

We cannot progressively make ourselves more acceptable to God so that He decides we are then 'fit for use'. It is only because in Christ He has definitively, irreversibly and graciously taken us to Himself, for Himself, making us His own, that we will live for His glory. If we are to grow more *like* Christ, we must first take hold of the glorious truth of what we have already become *in Christ*.[10]

DEAD TO SIN
In Romans chapter 6 Paul expounds this truth and applies it to the life of the believer. The chapter is written in response to the question raised in verse 1: 'Are we to continue in sin that grace may abound?' Paul's response is full of what we might call 'gospel incredulity': 'How can we who died to sin still live in it?' The very idea is outrageous and incomprehensible.

A fact of the past: baptized into Christ
The phrase 'died to sin' is a reference to the power and tyrannical rule of sin. As believers, we are now no longer

---

9   David Peterson, *Possessed by God, A New Testament Theology of Sanctification and Holiness*, p. 14.

10   For more on this, John Murray, 'Definitive Sanctification', cited previously, is worthwhile.

'in Adam' but 'in Christ'. We have been taken out of sin's sphere. We are no longer under its rule or subject to its authority. So it is not, in the first instance, a reference to our experience. There is a thrilling objectivity to it. It is a statement of fact, irrespective of our emotional awareness. It is this fact that makes the question posed by Paul one of incredulity. How can sin be normative for those of us who have died to it? How can we who belong to that category of people who are 'in Christ' live as though we are functionally 'in Adam'? It is so absurd as to be unthinkable.

In Romans 6:3-5, Paul unambiguously unites believers with Christ in His death, burial and resurrection:

> Do you not know that all of us who have been baptised into Christ Jesus were baptised into his death? We were buried therefore with him by baptism into death, in order that, just as Christ was raised from the dead by the glory of the Father, we too might walk in newness of life. For if we have been united with him in a death like his, we shall certainly be united with him in a resurrection like his.

Christ died, was buried, and rose from the dead. But He was not alone! All who enjoy this union with Him by the Spirit also died, were buried, and rose again to a new life. Paul uses their baptism as his reference point. Baptism is a piece of gospel drama. It tells the story of redemption. It rehearses not only what happened to Christ in time and space, but also what has happened to every believer. Baptism is God's provision for how we respond to the gospel.

In baptism, we are to remember not only objective historical facts, but the great existential reality: we have been rescued. The Spirit is so intimately involved in taking

all that Christ did, applying it to us and bringing us into
Christ that it is a real and dynamic relationship. We are
partakers of all of these triumphal achievements. Satan
doesn't want us to believe that. He wants us to feel isolated
and sorry for ourselves – to wallow in our self-pity so
that temptation becomes more attractive to us. Yet our
union with Christ as His people is so intimate that we are
partakers with Him in all of His victorious achievements
in His death, burial and resurrection.

Therefore, the call of progressive or transformative sanctification is simply this: to be who we are! When Satan tempts
us, we are to remind him not only of his past (that he was
defeated at the cross); we are to remind him also of *our* past at
the cross. We have moved out of Satan's authority. All he can
do is insinuate, try and beguile; but in actuality, he is powerless.
We stand in Christ because of our union with Christ.

A response in the present: consider yourselves dead to sin
In Romans 6:6, Paul writes about the 'old self' being
crucified with Christ. That has happened. That old,
rebellious humanity – of which each of us was once a card-
carrying, fully participating member – is now dead to us.[11]
As we said earlier in the chapter, it is no longer the 'sphere'
in which we operate. This is why we are no longer enslaved
to sin: for the simple reason that 'the one who has died is
freed from sin' (v. 7).

The logic seems compelling, not least because of the
word 'for' that starts the sentence. But because the word
translated 'freed' (v. 7) is the word that is often translated

---

11 Paul is not talking about each of us having two natures that are in some
    way in conflict with each other; the 'old self' and the 'new self'. The old
    self is the 'in Adam' self which no longer exists.

'justified', in what sense is the believer who has died with Christ freed from sin? Is Paul talking about our being 'acquitted from the penalty of sin', or 'liberated from the domination of sin'? It seems that Paul answers this in verse 18: 'You have been set free from sin and have become slaves to righteousness.' It is sin's domination that is in view here. This fits perfectly with what Paul has already said in verses 1-2. Paul is saying that we have been liberated from sin's power. Not only have we escaped from our deserved punishment for sin, we are also no longer dominated by sin. Indeed, in chapter 8:1-4, Paul will go on to show that the Spirit's work in setting us free from the law of sin and death by uniting us with Christ not only guarantees us shelter from God's judgement: it also enables us now to fulfil the Law's requirements.

Back in chapter 6, Paul turns in verse 11 to underline what our response must be to our union with Christ in His death and resurrection: 'So you also must consider yourselves dead to sin and alive to God in Christ Jesus.'

The word translated 'so' or 'in the same way' connects us to what has gone before. Because of our union with Christ we have died to sin (v. 10), and we have risen so that we might walk in newness of life (v. 4). By dying to sin, Christ defeated sin and death. His resurrection was the seal and fruit of that victory, and the necessary promise of future life for believers. His death was a victory. There is a view of the crucifixion that sees it as a point of defeat. That is profoundly wrong. When Jesus cried out, 'It is finished!' it was a cry of victory. The resurrection didn't take Satan by surprise; he was already conquered at Calvary. Calvin writes this in his commentary on Colossians 2:16, which occurs in a passage that is very close in thought to this chapter:

For although in the cross there is nothing but curse, it was, nevertheless, swallowed up by the power of God in such a way, that it has put on, as it were, a new nature. For there is no tribunal so magnificent, no throne so stately, no show of triumph so distinguished, no chariot so elevated as is the gibbet on which Christ has subdued death and the devil, the prince of death; nay more, has utterly trodden them under his feet.[12]

That is how effective and decisive the cross is in the purposes of God. By expounding our union with Christ, Paul locates us firmly in that cosmic event to show how effective and decisive it is for us.

Paul says, therefore, that we are to 'consider [ourselves] *dead* to sin'. This command is not a case of 'mind over matter' or 'positive thinking'. Paul is calling us to thinking which is based in reality. We are to understand and *consider* what is true of us. If we want to live as though we belong to a category of those who have died to sin, if we want to be who we are, we must think about ourselves in the light of reality. We must think about what is actually true of us. This is not what *might* be true of us, or what is true of us in *some* circumstances but not others. No, this is what is true of us in Christ. The reality for Christians is that, in Christ, we have died to sin.

... AND ALIVE TO GOD

All of this does not mean that we cannot sin anymore. We know only too well that that is not the case. But sin is no longer our master. We no longer live under the sphere of its authority. We are like secret agents in enemy territory – we are in the country, but not obeying its rule because the

---

12   John Calvin, *Commentaries*, Volume XLII, Colossians ch. 2 v. 16.

territory has no authority over us. As a British person, for example, France has no authority over me to pay its taxes. If I receive a letter informing me that I have taxes due to France, I could rip it up because I am not under French authority. It is irrelevant to me. In Christ we are dead to sin and alive to God: sin has no authority over us at all. That is our current condition.

Paul is exhorting us to recognise, appreciate, and live in the light of that reality. One of our biggest problems in sanctification is that we refuse to recognise who we are in Christ. We don't appreciate the radical, all-encompassing nature of our identity in Christ. We read about His death and resurrection as if it simply happened to Him. It did happen to Him of course, but not *just* to Him. It happened to us. This is why Paul develops his argument still further in Romans 6:12-14:

> Let not sin therefore reign in your mortal body, to make you obey its passions. Do not present your members to sin as instruments for unrighteousness, but present yourselves to God as those who have been brought from death to life, and your members to God as instruments for righteousness.

Paul can issue those commands and present that lifestyle as a viable option for us only because of our union with Christ. Our problem is that we get to the point where we think that sin is irresistible. That is a lie from Satan himself. The life-changing news for the believer is that, because we are in Christ, sin is never inevitable for us. In 1 Corinthians 10:13, Paul writes: 'No temptation has overtaken you except what is common to mankind. And God is faithful; He will not let you be tempted beyond what you can bear. But when you are tempted, he will also provide a way out so that you can endure it' (NIV). Whatever our circumstances, we are easily convinced that no one has been through what we are going through. No one has had that much money, or had a co-worker quite as attractive as that, or a child quite so difficult.

That circumstance, whatever it is, is a *temptation*: Satan is using it to cause us to sin. That same circumstance, however, is also a *trial*: God is using it to cause us to grow more like His Son. Satan is saying, 'You know you deserve it: go for it!' He wants you to dishonour God. But the Spirit is saying, 'You know who you are in Christ; you know you don't have to do that. I've put you in this situation so that you might see who you are in Christ, and run to Him.'

When we are tempted, God's intention is always that we become fit for purpose. Whether we are being badly treated by our employers, or our kids are driving us crazy; whether it's the pop-up that appears on the computer screen, or the opportunity to put someone down and get some laughs for ourselves: we can have confidence that sin is not inevitable, and that God is at work in that situation, calling and wooing us to pursue Christ and to find our identity in Him alone. We are united with Christ in His death and resurrection. In every situation, therefore, we are to count ourselves dead to sin and alive to God: to the one who is working intimately in us to transform us into the image of His Son.

CONCLUSION

What might this look like in practice? Imagine a fellow Christian you know called Jonny. He's come to you to say he's struggling with porn. He's made some attempts to stop a few times, but he keeps going back to it. How would you help him to grasp the life-changing reverberations of his union with Christ? Three principles might help us here.

1. Remind people that they died with Christ: they are no longer 'in Adam'

This is both a call and a comfort. Because he was crucified with Christ, it is no longer consistent for Jonny to live as if he were 'in Adam': his identity in Christ is a call to count himself dead to sin. Jonny is to repent, and to do everything he can to put sin to death with all the strength Christ gives him through the Spirit.

His identity in Christ is not just a call to godliness: it is also a great comfort. Because he was crucified with Christ, Jonny is no longer 'in Adam', and so sin no longer has any dominion over him. When we counsel people, we're always telling them good news: we're not simply telling people that they 'shouldn't' sin, but that they 'don't need to' sin because of some aspect of the gospel. You can encourage Jonny that he doesn't have to turn to porn, because he is no longer 'in Adam': sin no longer reigns over him.

2. Remind people of their new identity: they are now in Christ

Because Jonny has been raised with Christ, he is not just freed from sin: he has become a 'slave to righteousness'! He has a new identity and a new power for godliness through the Spirit. You can encourage Jonny that God is working even in his temptations to draw him to Christ, and to pursue Christ with all the strength that the Spirit gives him.

3. Show people how being in Christ is better than being in Adam

Finally, you can show Jonny how Christ is better than sin: that his union with Christ and the relationship he has with Christ in the Spirit are more real and lasting than the 'fleeting pleasures of sin' (Heb. 11:25). You can help Jonny to meditate on the glorious forgiveness there is in Christ through the cross, on all the riches there are in Him, and on the wonderful future that is coming, so that he will begin to see sin as the paltry, pathetic thing that it is.

Four

Together in Christ

Imagine this: James, a man in your church, has been a believer for a couple of years. He appears to be growing in Christ and is a real contributor to the life of the church. You only begin to spot the signs that all is not right when one afternoon you see him in the distance in a nearby shopping mall. You lose sight of him again, and so call him on his mobile to see if he wants to go for a coffee.

'Hi, how are you doing?' you say as he picks up the phone.

'Oh fine,' he says. 'I'm at work, so I can't talk for long.'

This is obviously untrue. But when you challenge him, he replies defensively that he meant to say that he was out shopping, and changes the subject. Over the next few weeks and months, however, it becomes obvious that James has a fairly free attitude to truth, and that others in the church are talking about it too. You decide you'll go for a walk with James, and pray for an opportunity to talk about the issue.

How would you counsel James? To what truths would you take him? Perhaps you would seek to show him that God is a God of truth, and so lying is inappropriate for those who belong to him. Or maybe you would take him to the Ten Commandments and to God's prohibition against bearing false witness.

In Ephesians 4:25, Paul is dealing with this same issue. But his methods are striking. 'Therefore, having put away falsehood, let each of you speak the truth with his neighbour, for we are members of one another.' Paul appeals not to God's character, nor to God's commands, but to the reality of believers' union with Christ and with one another. Union with Christ is foundational to all Christian thinking and living. This is no less true for the life of the church, the body of Christ.

In Ephesians, the apostle demonstrates both the cosmic grandeur of what it means to be the church in Christ, and the very day-to-day applications of that doctrine for the local church. As we trace this theme through the letter, we will notice how Paul sees an understanding of their union with Christ as both essential and fundamentally transformative for the shared life of the churches which he is addressing.

THE CHURCH: UNITED IN CHRIST

On 9th November 1989 the Berlin Wall came down. After over forty years of division Germany was now no longer divided in two, but was one nation. Families who had been separated by that great dividing wall were reunited, amid scenes of joy and jubilation.

In Ephesians chapter 2 Paul describes a reunification far greater even than this. In the opening lines of his letter

Paul has already laid out the comprehensive blessings that belong to believers by virtue of their union with Christ. He has then prayed that God will enlighten the hearts of those he's addressing so that they'll grasp the riches of all they have in Christ. Next he has begun to describe the magnitude of the change that has taken place in believers in Christ. In the first half of the chapter he has described how they have moved from being dead in sins to being alive in Christ, and from being under the power of the devil to being seated with Christ in the heavenly places. He has portrayed how they have been transformed from being those in slavery to their sinful desires to being those created in Christ Jesus to do good works. In the second half of the chapter, however, he continues to explain the great change that has taken place in believers through their union with Christ. But here he views that change not in terms of what has happened to individual believers, but in terms of what has happened to humanity as a whole.

He begins by reminding the Ephesians of the great dividing wall that cut through humanity prior to Christ's coming:

> Therefore remember that at one time you Gentiles in the flesh, called 'the uncircumcision' by what is called the circumcision, which is made in the flesh by hands— remember that you were at that time separated from Christ, alienated from the commonwealth of Israel and strangers to the covenants of promise, having no hope and without God in the world. (Eph. 2:11-12)

Divided we fall

His point is clear: before Christ, Gentiles were cut off from being part of God's people. They were 'alienated from the

commonwealth of Israel'. Not only this, they were excluded
from relationship with God: they were 'separated from
Christ' and 'strangers to the covenants of promise, having
no hope and without God in the world'. The wall in the
Jerusalem temple between the court of the Gentiles and
the inner courts of the Jews was the great symbol of this
division: it stood about four feet six inches high and had
written on it the menacing inscription: 'Whoever is arrested
will himself be responsible for his death, which will follow.'
They could have no fellowship with God's people, and no
fellowship with God: the wall could not be breached.

This was not the only dividing wall, however. In verse
16, Paul speaks of the need for Christ to 'reconcile us both
to God'. Both Jews and Gentiles were cut off from God.
Gentiles were cut off by virtue of their exclusion from the
promises of God. Jews were cut off by dint of their sin and
disobedience. The dividing wall between Jews and God
stood not at the entrance to the inner courts, but at the
entrance to the Holy of Holies in the form of a great sixty-
foot-high curtain which screened off the presence of the
holy God from His sinful people. Paul's picture is striking:
a humanity cut off from God and divided from one another.

United we stand

What follows, however, is breath-taking. In Christ,
through the cross, God has created a whole new humanity:

> But now in Christ Jesus you who once were far off
> have been brought near by the blood of Christ. For he
> himself is our peace, who has made us both one and has
> broken down in his flesh the dividing wall of hostility
> by abolishing the law of commandments expressed in
> ordinances, that he might create in himself one new man

in place of the two, so making peace, and might reconcile
us both to God in one body through the cross, thereby
killing the hostility. And he came and preached peace to
you who were far off and peace to those who were near.
For through him we both have access in one Spirit to the
Father. (Eph. 2:13-18)

What God has effected in Christ is more than simply
a privatised, individual salvation. In Christ, God has done
something of global magnitude. In Christ, through the
cross, God has 'brought near' those who were 'far off'.
He has 'made us both one'. He has 'broken down in His
flesh the dividing wall of hostility by abolishing the law
of commandments expressed in ordinances.' Through His
law-fulfilling life and wrath-absorbing death, Christ has
done away with every barrier. The Law now no longer
stands as a barrier between Jews and God, or between
Jews and Gentiles. Both Jews and Gentiles have been
reconciled 'to God in one body through the cross'.

But what is God's purpose in all of this? Verse 15 tells
us: '... that he might create in himself one new man out
of the two, so making peace, and might reconcile us both
to God in one body through the cross'. The word Paul
uses for 'man' is the Greek word *anthrōpos*, which means
'humanity'. Through His death on the cross, Christ has
created in Himself a whole new humanity: reconciled to
God and to one another.

The explicit 'union with Christ' language here is emphatic:
'*in Christ* Jesus you ... have been brought near' (v. 13); '*he
himself* is our peace' (v. 14); 'that he might create *in himself* one
new man' (v. 15); 'and might reconcile us both to God *in one
body*' (v. 16). Christ is not simply the means by which we have
been brought peace: He Himself is our peace.

Not only this, but the metaphors Paul uses to describe this new humanity grow increasingly intimate and essential as he continues. First, Gentiles are 'no longer strangers and aliens, but ... are fellow-citizens with the saints' (2:19a): this new humanity is a new reconciled *people of God*. Next, Gentiles and Jews are together 'members of the household of God' (2:19b): because they are in Christ the Son, they are brothers and sisters in *God's family*. Third, they are 'being joined together' (2:22) into *a temple* where God dwells by the Spirit, 'Christ Jesus himself being the cornerstone' (2:20): they are stones so expertly hewn and chiselled that they fit together perfectly as a dwelling place for God Himself. Finally, in chapter 4 the metaphors reach their climax as Paul describes the church as 'the body of Christ' (4:12). The relationship between Christ and the church is as essential as the relationship between a head and its body: you can no more think of Christ without the church than you can think of a head without a body. Not only this, but the relationship between believers is as essential as the relationship between the different parts of a body: the body can grow and function as intended only when it is 'joined and held together by every joint with which it is equipped', and 'when each part is working properly' (4:16). Because we are united with Christ, we are inextricably united with all those who are also united with Him. The church belongs to Christ; Christ belongs to the church; and those who are in Christ belong to one another.

An understanding of our union with Christ is therefore essential to all our thinking about the church. The church – God's new humanity united in Christ – is God's ultimate goal for His creation. What does all this mean? Paul draws out the comprehensive implications in the rest of his letter.

THE CHURCH: A COSMIC DISPLAY OF GOD'S WISDOM
IN CHRIST

At the London Olympics in 2012 Britain had an
opportunity to display its glory to the world. In an
interview with *The Sunday Telegraph* during the Games,
Mayor of London Boris Johnson said: 'The most important
thing about the Olympics is that they have shown that
Britain really can do things ... We have shown the world
we are a happy, ambitious, modern, successful economy.'[1]
For Johnson and other British politicians, the Olympic
Games were a technicolor display of the glories of Britain
before all the powers of the world.

In Ephesians chapter 3 Paul says that the church in
Christ is a display far more magnificent than this: it is
God's own display of His multicoloured wisdom before
the powers of the whole universe.

> To me, though I am the very least of all the saints,
> this grace was given, to preach to the Gentiles the
> unsearchable riches of Christ, and to bring to light for
> everyone what is the plan of the mystery hidden for
> ages in God who created all things, so that through
> the church the manifold wisdom of God might now be
> made known to the rulers and authorities in the heavenly
> places. This was according to the eternal purpose that he
> has realised in Christ Jesus our Lord ... (Eph. 3:8-11)

Through the church 'the manifold wisdom of God' is
'made known' (3:10). The word translated 'manifold' here
(*polupoikilos*) means 'multi-coloured', and was used in the

---

1   http://www.telegraph.co.uk/news/politics/conservative/9469376/
    Boris-Johnson-tells-David-Cameron-to-go-for-growth-to-harness-
    Olympic-legacy.html

ancient world of things such as flowers, embroidered cloth and woven carpets.[2] The church is made up of people from all races, cultures, backgrounds and colours now reconciled in Christ. And here Paul is saying something spectacular about this new humanity: the multi-coloured church in Christ is a public display of the multi-coloured wisdom of God. The church is God's own evidence that the cross worked!

And yet it is not simply a display of God's wisdom to *human* onlookers. The church in Christ is the demonstration of the reconciliation Christ has won '*to the rulers and authorities in the heavenly places*' (3:10). Paul probably has in mind here both the good and the bad spiritual powers: both angels and demons. As the billions of worshipping angels look on at the church being gathered from every nation under heaven, they rejoice in the glorious, tangible fruit of all that God has achieved in Christ. Conversely, as 'the spiritual forces of evil in the heavenly places' (6:12) look on at the same reality, they see the unmistakeable sign that all their plots have failed: the 'eternal purpose that [God] has realised in Christ Jesus our Lord' (3:11) is being brought to fruition in the church. In chapter 1 Paul has told us that one day God will 'unite all things in [Christ], things in heaven and things on earth' (1:10). The devil's schemes will one day come to an end as everything in the universe is reconciled under Christ's gracious lordship. Today, the multi-racial church reconciled in Christ stands as a beautiful time-and-space anticipation of that final day.

Why does Paul tell the Ephesians this? Why do we in our churches today need to recapture this same vision of

---

2   John Stott, *The Message of Ephesians* (IVP, 1979), p.123.

the church in Christ? One reason is that such a cosmic view of the church will utterly transform your attitude to your local church.

Imagine that you are part of a small church-plant of just ten adults and a gaggle of children in an obscure town in rural England. You're an unspectacular group of people, with more than your fair share of idiosyncrasies, differences, weaknesses, illnesses and sin. You're not seeing enormous numbers of conversions. You don't even always all get along. Because of all this, it would be easy to think that this isn't really where it's at: that what God is doing in His world must be somewhere other than here. It would be tempting to go looking for a spiritual experience or 'life to the full' elsewhere: in a more dynamic church, in a more 'happening' setting, or even outside of God's people altogether. And yet Paul is saying in Ephesians 2-3 that this is precisely 'where it's at': here, in this fledgling church made up of losers like you, God is displaying His multi-coloured wisdom to the universe. 'Do you want to see what I've done in my Son?' says God to the rulers and authorities in the heavenly realms. 'Then look at this beautiful, rag-tag bunch of sinners that I've bought and brought together in Him!'

Church life is messy. It's tough, it's long and it's often ugly. That's why we need to help each other to regain God's own view of His church: we are a people reconciled in Christ to display His wisdom to the universe.

The church: a body growing in Christ
In Ephesians 4:1 Paul begins to tell the Ephesians what it will mean to live out their identity in Christ in the context of their day-to-day lives: he urges them 'to walk in a manner worthy of the calling to which you have been

called'. Chapters 1–3 have been full of glorious indicatives about what Christ has done and who they are in Him. Chapters 4–6 are full of glorious imperatives instructing the Ephesians how they are to 'walk out' those wonderful indicatives in their lives.

Paul is clear from the beginning, however, that, for the Ephesians, living out their identity in Christ will not be an individual pursuit. Rather, they are to walk 'with all humility and gentleness, with patience, bearing with one another in love, eager to maintain the unity of the Spirit in the bond of peace' (4:2-3). Their identity is a corporate identity: in Christ, they already have 'the unity of the Spirit' and 'the bond of peace'. Walking out that identity will therefore be a corporate endeavour, as they seek 'to maintain' the unity they have in Christ and to live it out before a watching world.

What will this look like? Paul's first point is that living out our corporate identity will mean living as a body which is growing together in Christ.

Steve and Rebecca became Christians through an evangelistic Bible course. They loved the course and everything about it, and so they were enthusiastic about inviting friends along to the next one, which they hosted in their home. But somehow they never made the transition to being committed members of a local church. They went along to the meetings fairly consistently, but they never really built relationships with other believers. Chatting in bed about it late one night, Rebecca said to Steve, 'I really enjoy the sermons at church, but I just find that reading the Bible on my own is the most helpful way of growing to know Jesus more. And it's not like I'm not witnessing: I get loads of opportunities to talk about Jesus at work!'

What would you say to Steve and Rebecca? In chapter 4:15-16, Paul tells the Ephesians:

> Rather, speaking the truth in love, we are to grow up in every way into him who is the head, into Christ, from whom the whole body, joined and held together by every joint with which it is equipped, when each part is working properly, makes the body grow so that it builds itself up in love.

Paul's point is two-fold. First, the *goal* of our life in Christ is not so much that we grow as individuals, but that the 'whole body' grows up 'into him who is the head, into Christ'. When I grasp my union with Christ and with the other members of His body, I can no longer think of my life as simply being about my own personal growth in godliness: my life is about helping the body to grow together in Christ. God's intention is to have a people who love His Son and who love one another radically from the heart. 'Spiritual growth' when living as an isolated individual is not really spiritual growth at all – growth in Christ by the Spirit will always mean growth in love for my brothers and sisters. Steve and Rebecca may look like they are growing in Christ, but in reality they are not. They need a fresh vision of the reality of their union with Christ and with their fellow believers if they are to be brought into the fullness of all that God has saved them for in Christ.

Second, the *way* the body grows is as each part of the body does its work. In a body, the growth of each part depends on the proper functioning of the other parts. If the feet are not working properly, all the other members will be adversely affected. In the same way, Christ's body grows as each member functions as it should. In Ephesians 4:7 Paul has already told us that 'grace was given to each one of us according to the measure of Christ's gift'. In His kindness, Christ has graciously given each member of His body particular 'grace-gifts' that are necessary for the building up of His body. 'Every joint', every member, is necessary for the body to grow properly. It is by the various members of the body 'speaking the truth in love' in a myriad of ways that the body 'builds itself up in love'. The profound reality of our union with Christ means that the local church needs Steve and Rebecca if that local expression of Christ's body is to grow as it should; and Steve and Rebecca need the ministry of the other members of the church if they are to grow as they should.

THE CHURCH: A FAMILY RELATING IN CHRIST

The implications of being united with Christ and with one another, however, are not limited to the area of our mutual edification. Rather, they extend into every area of our life together in Christ. In 4:17–6:9 Paul lays out the ways in which the reality of the Ephesians' union with Christ will transform them into a community of light whose lives will stand in stark contrast to the 'dis-community of darkness' among which they live. At the heart of this transformation will be an ongoing and determined effort: '[putting] off your old self' and '[putting] on the new self, created after the likeness of God in true righteousness and holiness' (4:22-24). The word Paul uses for 'self' here is the same word (*anthrōpos*) that he uses in 2:15 to describe the new humanity that God has created in Christ through the cross. Paul is explicitly calling the Ephesians not to live out of their old identity as those separated from God and from one another, but instead to 'be who they are': a new humanity reconciled in Christ.

What will this look like? In 4:25-32 Paul highlights six ways in which the Ephesians' union with Christ and with one another will transform their lives.

First, when they grasp that they are 'members of one another' they will no longer lie to one another, but each one will 'speak the truth with his neighbour' (4:25). To do anything else would be to live in contradiction to their belonging to one another in Christ.

Second, they must resolve conflict quickly, in order to 'give no opportunity to the devil' (4:26-27). We have already seen that the church's union with Christ and with one another is a cosmic slap in the face for the devil and his minions in their attempts to bring division and disharmony (3:10). Paul appeals to the Ephesians to live out this identity by dealing with conflict quickly, thus removing all opportunity for the devil to sow division once more.

Third, the one who stole must no longer steal, but must do 'honest work with his hands, so that he may have something to share with anyone in need' (4:28). The reality of his union with Christ and with his fellow believers will mean that the thief does not simply give up stealing from his brothers and sisters, but actually works hard to provide for those in his family in Christ who are struggling.

Fourth, they must not use 'corrupting talk', but instead say only that which 'is good for building up' (4:29). The corporate nature of their union with Christ must so shape them that everything they say is affected by their desire to see the body of Christ growing in love for Him and for one another.

Fifth, they must get rid of 'all bitterness and wrath and anger and clamour and slander' (4:31) from among them.

Why? Because this would 'grieve the Holy Spirit of God, by whom [they] were sealed for the day of redemption' (4:30). The Spirit has united them with Christ and sealed them for Him – to live with bitterness and anger towards one another would be to live as if the Spirit had not graciously done this work in their lives.

Finally, they must forgive one another, 'as in Christ God forgave you' (4:32). In Christ, they have been forgiven (1:7) and reconciled to God (2:16). Their lives must therefore display this wonderful reality: their ongoing forgiveness of one another is to be modelled on and empowered by the way God has forgiven them in Christ.

Paul is emphatic: what our churches need, if they are to thrive, is neither more programmes nor more strategies. What we as believers need, if we are to grow in love for one another and display our precious Jesus to the world, is not a list of relationship techniques and tips. Rather, we need a deep and vital understanding and experience of our union with Christ and with one another in Him.

THE CHURCH: A LIGHT SHINING CHRIST TO THE WORLD

Imagine a friend invites you to see your local football club play, as they've just appointed a new manager. The team are useless, and have plummeted through the divisions. Manager after manager has come, but it makes no difference: the team can't pass, they can't tackle, and they can't shoot. Your friend is insistent, however, that this new manager is different: he's really someone special. So you reluctantly agree to go with him to see the game, mainly because he's offered to buy you a pie at half-time. But what you see is astounding. The team are unrecognisably good. They pass. They tackle. They play together. They shoot.

They defend as a unit. By half-time the score is 5-0. These are the same players as before, playing on the same pitch, with the same fans watching. But the transformation is unbelievable. There's only one explanation: this new manager really is a miracle-worker. How do you know? Because you've seen what he's done with a team of selfish, good-for-nothing no-hopers.

In Ephesians 5:11-14 Paul gives this tantalising picture to the Ephesian Christians to spur them on in their communal pursuit of godliness:

> Take no part in the unfruitful works of darkness, but instead expose them. For it is shameful even to speak of the things that they do in secret. But when anything is exposed by the light, it becomes visible, for anything that becomes visible is light. Therefore it says,
> 'Awake, O sleeper, and arise from the dead,
> and Christ will shine on you.'

This is an inspiring vision. As believers we are to show up the darkness and evil of the world around us. We do this, however, not primarily through our words denouncing those around us, but through our lives together 'as children of light' (5:8): as we live out our corporate identity in Christ. And the result is spectacular: people currently living in darkness and death will 'arise from the dead' (v. 14). The last time we heard the language of death and life in Ephesians was in chapter 2:1-5, where Paul described the work that God had done in the Ephesians' lives in bringing them from being dead in their sins to being alive in Christ. Here he says the same of those living around the Ephesians: some of them will 'arise from the dead' – they will be given spiritual life! How will this happen? Through the believers' relationships of love and purity, 'Christ will shine on [them]'.

What Paul is saying here is nothing short of spectacular. As unbelievers hear the gospel message and see this group of selfish, good-for-nothing no-hopers who have been united in Christ and are being transformed by the Spirit, Christ Himself will shine on them, and some will be brought from death to life. God's intention is to use the corporate life of His people in Christ to shine on men and women currently living in darkness and death, and to authenticate the gospel message they are hearing and thereby draw them into life and faith in His Son Jesus.

Conclusion

In our church we say often that we want to shine like a light in the darkness around us. We want to grow in our love for Christ and for one another. We want to become a community where we forgive quickly, give sacrificially and speak the truth to one another in love. We want our neighbours, colleagues, friends and family to spend time among us, and not only to hear the gospel, but also to experience a group of people whose relationships can be explained only by the truth of that gospel. If we wish to see all this, then we need to help each other to understand with our minds and to grasp with our hearts the beautiful reality of our union with Christ and with one another in Him. Following the apostle Paul's example, we need to help one another to work out the implications of that life-changing union in the everyday situations of our lives together.

Five

On Mission in Christ

As those who are 'in Christ', our identity is radically different from our previous identity as those 'in Adam'. As we have seen, we are no longer who we once were. We are now ingrafted into the vine, adopted into God's family, one with Christ in His life, death and resurrection. This new identity has a profound influence on how we view mission.

MOTIVATION FOR MISSION

Because of our union with Christ, our lives are no longer our own. We have been bought with a price – we belong to the Saviour who has wooed us, won our hearts and brought us from death to life. J. Todd Billings explains the totality of our union with Christ:

We would rather have the occasional brush of God's presence, or a relic of his solidarity with us, so that God can be an appendage of our identity. But God wants more than that; he wants our lives, our adopted identity ... By bringing us into the new reality of the Spirit, we can call out to God – Abba, Father – as adopted children united to Christ. Yet there are few things more countercultural than this process of adoption – losing your life for the sake of Jesus Christ, to find it in communion with the Triune God.[1]

A passion for God's glory

God wants what is His: all that we are and have. This belongs to Him by virtue of creation but, even more significantly, by virtue of redemption: He has purchased us for Himself. As those who are united with Christ, and who are therefore sons of God who belong to Him in His family, our hearts are stirred for His glory. Our ambition is to proclaim the gospel of Jesus to all the nations, gathering His people from among every tongue and tribe. Because of our new identity, God's mission is our mission. We are those who have lost our lives in Christ and for Christ. We are those who find our lives in Christ and for Christ.

A compassion for men's souls

We preach the gospel because God's mission is our mission, and because our hearts are stirred for His glory. But, as those in Christ, we also preach the gospel out of compassion for the plight of those who are still outside of Christ. 2 Corinthians 5:14-21 is a clear example of how Paul's identity in Christ compelled him to preach the gospel:

---

1   J. Todd Billings, *Union with Christ: Reframing Theology and Ministry for the Church* (Baker Academic, 2012), p. 18.

For Christ's love compels us, because we are convinced that one died for all, and therefore all died. And he died for all, that those who live should no longer live for themselves but for him who died for them and was raised again. So from now on we regard no one from a worldly point of view. Though we once regarded Christ in this way, we do so no longer. Therefore, if anyone is *in Christ*, the new creation has come: The old has gone, the new is here! All this is from God, who reconciled us to himself through Christ and gave us the ministry of reconciliation: that God was reconciling the world to himself *in Christ*, not counting people's sins against them. And he has committed to us the message of reconciliation. We are therefore Christ's ambassadors, as though God were making his appeal through us. We implore you on Christ's behalf: Be reconciled to God. God made him who had no sin to be sin for us, so that *in him* we might become the righteousness of God. [NIV; author's italics]

Paul says that because we are in Christ, we are Christ's ambassadors – God appeals to lost sinners through us. Because we have known reconciliation with God in Christ, we implore the world around us, on Christ's behalf, to be reconciled to God. Our identity in Christ is what qualifies us to share the gospel and compels us to do so. We have known such grace, such mercy, such unmerited favour, such unbounded blessing in Christ that our hearts are full of compassion for the lost world around us. All outside of Christ are dead in sin and without hope: we cannot be united with Christ and feel no compassion. As we recognise and embrace this identity of being one with our Saviour, our hearts will beat in time with His and know compassion for those who don't know Jesus.

IDENTITY, PURPOSE, FUNCTION

Our identity in Christ does not simply motivate us for mission: it also shows up our false motives in mission. The apostle Paul's gospel work was driven by his identification with Christ. As we have seen, the imperatives of the gospel (what we do for Christ) always flow from the indicatives of the gospel (who we are in Christ). Because we are in Christ, we preach the gospel. If we attempt to preach Christ from any other starting point we will soon fail, burdened by the weight of our legalism. Paul's zeal for preaching the gospel flows directly from the radical impact of union with Christ in his life.

As we think how our union with Christ reverberates into our missionary activity, the framework of *Identity, Purpose* and *Function* may be a helpful one.

IDENTITY (*WHO* I AM)

Our identity is 'in Christ'. It is 'in Christ' that we are forgiven, justified, blessed, adopted, set free, chosen, indwelt by the Holy Spirit, heading for glory. That is our identity; that is who we are. We don't need to secure or earn anything. We don't need to achieve or perform. There is nothing more to acquire. We cannot be anything more than we already are. This is good news. Every man or woman needs to know the answer to the question, 'Who am I?' In fact, we live our lives answering that question. All of our ambitions and achievements are not simply about what we do, but who we are. Our role in life and society defines us and so identifies us:

- I not only play football, but I am a footballer.

- I not only marry, but I am a wife.

- I not only have children, but I am a father.

- I not only run a company, but I am a successful businesswoman.

- I not only teach the Bible, but I am a preacher and Christian leader.

At one level, there is no problem with this. But when my role becomes my *identity*, then everything I have is invested in it, and so everything I am is dependent upon it. If my sense of worth and significance is found in running a business and the business fails, much more than my standard of living fails. If my sense of worth and significance is found in being a good father and one of my children rebels, much more than my relationship fails.

But 'in Christ' we now know who we are. We have an identity that is ours by grace. The pressure is off. The wonderful truth is that this actually liberates me to be a *better* businesswoman, wife, father or citizen! Any other role I have does not define me and so cannot control me, which means I am free to pursue each of those roles in ways that glorify God rather than demand 'success'.

This identity is the only thing that gives lasting motivation for mission, because it motivates by way of love rather than duty. We don't proclaim Christ in order to secure our place in heaven – sharing the gospel is not a prerequisite for earning God's favour. Rather, we share the gospel because we have freely received a new life, name, home and identity in Christ. Our motivation for action is the favour that has been so freely given to us through Jesus.

The term 'mission' includes both high-risk international mission in countries which are hostile towards Christianity, and sharing the gospel with your next-door neighbour in safe suburbia. It includes relocating to the deprived part of town to help start a church, and speaking God's truth to your colleagues at work. Whatever the situation or context, we are united to Christ and so we are all missionaries – because He was.

Purpose (*Why* I am)

If people struggle with the question, 'Who am I?', then we are equally troubled by the question, '*Why* am I?' As beings with the capacity for self-awareness who inhabit a large planet which is a mere speck in a vast universe, the question is inevitable. But the truth of our union with Christ provides us with a clear and emphatic answer. When God the Son became the Son of God, living the life that we could never live, He was preoccupied with His Father's glory. This was entirely appropriate because the Father was glorified in and through His Son. We are undoubtedly beneficiaries of the plan of salvation, but God is the primary object. His chief glory is in His grace that is ours in Christ. Yes, we are blessed when we respond in repentance and faith – but God is glorified, and that is His primary motivation. As those in Christ, that is also *our* 'chief end'.

Our purpose is to glorify God by making much of His Son. That is the overarching meaning of our lives, the secret of existence. As those in Christ we know why we are here and what we are here for. This purpose isn't a rod with which to beat us: it is a means of grace and the source of true satisfaction. But it is only known and enjoyed by those who are 'in Christ'. Outside of Him, there is ultimately only futility and confusion.

FUNCTION (*WHAT* I AM)

Our function is what we are called to be and do 'in the moment', in each and every circumstance no matter how extreme or diverse. As those in Christ our purpose is to glorify God through making much of His Son. Our function flows out of that identity and fulfils that purpose, and it is this: being lovers of God and lovers of others. We can ask ourselves in every situation, 'How can I love God and others best in this moment or circumstance?' That is our only concern, our primary responsibility. And because of who I am, I can face this challenge. God calls us and equips us, and has promised us all that we need for life and godliness.

CASE STUDIES

Being good neighbours

Jane and Andrew, newly married, had just moved into their first home. They loved it. It was a small two-bedroom house with a large garden and lots of potential. They settled to work painting, laying floors and carpets, clearing the wilderness that had grown up in the back garden and planting some vegetables, herbs and flowers. They started praying with their church group for their new neighbours, hoping to get to know them and share the gospel with them. Since Jane enjoyed baking, she knocked on doors with plates of biscuits as a friendly introduction, and they began planning a neighbourhood house-warming party. Everything seemed to be going well until the woman next door began treating them with inexplicable hostility. She accepted the plate of biscuits, but then dumped them over the back garden fence. She frowned and swore if Jane or Andrew said, 'Hello!' on the street. She slammed the door in his face when Andrew came round with the house-warming invitation. On top of that, she held loud parties late into the night, and the smell of cannabis often drifted over the fence into their garden and windows. Jane and Andrew were perplexed. They talked with their church group about what they should do: just ignore her and try to get on as best they could? Continue to be friendly while keeping a safe distance? Write a letter trying to get to the bottom of the problem, seeking resolution? Threaten to involve the police if the noise and drug use continued? How, they wondered, should they respond to this woman?

The motivation that led Jane and Andrew to reach out to their neighbours in the first place was their identity in Christ. Because they are united with Christ in His death and resurrection, their desires and priorities have changed to look more like the desires and priorities of their Lord. They know that their purpose is to glorify and enjoy God as they commend Jesus, so they seek to lift Him up in their behaviour towards their new neighbours. Finally, they know that their function is to love God and others moment by moment – this is where 'the rubber hits the road', so to speak. How do they love their awkward neighbour?

First, because their *identity* is firmly wrapped up in Jesus, what they do is not driven by the desire to placate or please their neighbour so that she has a better opinion of them. They are united with Christ Jesus, clothed in His righteousness and, with Him, heirs of eternal life. What anyone else thinks of them pales into insignificance.

This is very important. Think of the many times our behaviour towards someone comes from our desire for them to think well of us. It is a slavery from which we are freed through union with Christ. Because of union with Christ, their motivation to love this woman will be Christlike – selfless rather than self-centred.

Second, because their *purpose* is to glorify and enjoy God as they commend Jesus, their behaviour will be aligned with that all-encompassing reason for life. Their reason for existence is not to have a peaceful home, as enjoyable as that is. Their purpose is not to avoid conflict. Their purpose is not even to win their neighbours for Christ – that is a work only the Spirit can perform. Their purpose, which can only be accomplished in them through Christ, is simply to commend Jesus, and in so doing, glorify God. Whatever happens in this situation will not threaten their reason for living.

Finally, because of these two preliminary truths (their identity in Christ and purpose through Him), Andrew and Jane can *function* as intended. They are freed to truly love God and others, moment by moment. Their love for their neighbour is not driven by a fear of her opinion of them, or a desire just to 'get along'. Nor is it driven by thinking that they need anything (a perfect home, quiet nights, friendly neighbours) other than Jesus. Rather, their love for their neighbour will be compelled by Christ's love for them, and so it will be concerned with her best good.

Lack of fruit

Sarah is tired of living on New Street. She is tired of the manipulative relationships and the apathy to – and sometimes outright rejection of – the gospel message. She's weary of witnessing dysfunctional relationships and the gospel being ignored as the solution to that brokenness. She is beginning to wonder if she's cut out for this ministry: surely there are others who would be much more effective at explaining the gospel in a way that results in people becoming Christians, she thinks. In theory, she's happy to persevere – as long as the end result is conversions. The reality of seeing little visible gospel fruit after ten years, though, is beginning to take its toll. She wonders what the purpose of her being there is.

How does the reality of Sarah's union with Christ reverberate into this situation? First, Sarah can remember that she is 'in Christ'. Ephesians 1:3 says this: 'Blessed be the God and Father of our Lord Jesus Christ who has blessed us in Christ with every spiritual blessing ...' What are those blessings? Election. Predestination. Redemption. Forgiveness. Grace. Insight. Inheritance. Sealing. This is Sarah's defining *identity*. She is 'in Christ'; everything else is subsidiary. She is not first and foremost a man or a woman, a husband or wife, son or daughter, parent, lawyer, road cleaner, surgeon, teacher, refuse collector, politician or unemployed. She is not first and foremost a church planter or a minister, a PhD or a cutting-edge radical. She is, first and foremost, 'in Christ'.

For Sarah, her identity 'in Christ' will fill her with the liberating knowledge that her acceptance is not based on whether or not the people on her street become Christians. She is not first and foremost a gospel minister to needy people; she is first and foremost a beloved child of the King. This identity takes away the pressure. Yes, Sarah will be delighted if people accept Christ, but it will be because of the fame of Jesus rather than a validation of her as a gospel minister. Her joy and security do not depend on it. She can rest knowing that God has placed her in that mission field for a reason, regardless of whether others might appear to be more effective.

Second, Sarah's *purpose* is to glorify God by commending Christ: nothing more and nothing less. Her purpose is not to win converts or to be influential in seeing the gospel restore broken lives: her purpose is to glorify God by commending Christ in any and every situation. When she is feeling downcast by the lack of fruit, or questioning whether she's really the best woman for the job, remembering her purpose will refresh her. She is made to delight in Jesus, commending Him, and so glorifying the Father. That is her purpose, and, in Christ, she can be who she was made to be. She can, and must, leave everything else in her Father's hands, trusting God's sovereignty in her life.

Third, being a lover of God and others is what Sarah is made to do. In Christ, this is what she does. Remembering this simple core *function* will help Sarah when she feels burdened by the problems and cares of others. Her responsibility, at any given moment, is to love God and others – it isn't to fix everyone's problems. A helpful question for her to ask is: 'How do I love them – in this moment, in this instance?' This means that Sarah is able to make decisions that might not be popular. For instance, when the mum across the street – someone Sarah and her church group know closely – is abusing drugs and alcohol to the extent that her children are in danger, Sarah is able to love her well. She speaks openly to the mum, expressing that she cares for her and her kids, and that if the behaviour doesn't change she will have to call social services to protect them. The mum doesn't like it, but acknowledges to others that she knows Sarah did it because she cares. Because of her *identity* in Christ and her *purpose* in commending Jesus and glorifying God, Sarah's *function* of loving God and others is possible.

Persecution

Harry and Paula had been living in India for five years now, and things were beginning to heat up. When they had first arrived, the tiny group of local Christians had welcomed them with joyful eagerness. Harry and Paula were able to contribute to the work in tangible ways. And people were being saved! For the first three years, ministry was incredibly fruitful. Their prayer letters home were full of thanks. Then they received their first threat, a rough scribbled letter attached to a rock which was thrown through the window of their little church. Local leaders did not like the influence these Christians were beginning to have. A few weeks later, Harry received a notice that he would not be allowed to continue teaching. The women Paula had been reading the Bible with began quietly to become unavailable, frightened by taunts and threats from neighbours. They wondered what they should do: stay to see the local church fully established? Move to another area that would allow them freedom to share the gospel? When Harry was pushed over and kicked in the street one day, they began to wonder if they were taking too big a risk.

How might the truth of Harry and Paula's union with Christ reverberate into this situation?

First, the great encouragement is that Harry and Paula's identity in Christ is secure whatever they decide to do. If they decide to stay, they can stay with confidence, peace and hope because in Christ they have an eternal glory already secured. By God's grace they can face persecution, hardship and even death because, in Christ, it is not the end for them. If they decide to go, they go knowing that they are not lesser Christians. The union they have with Christ does not change depending on their actions because it is entirely God's work, through the Spirit, to claim and redeem them in Christ. We can never be loved any more or less by God than we are right now, in Christ.

Knowing that their *purpose* is to glorify God as they commend Jesus is, again, liberating. Harry and Paula's purpose is to make much of Jesus. They can do this whether they stay or go.

Their *function* as lovers of God and lovers of others helps to direct decisions. Harry and Paula's identity in Christ never changes. They live out their purpose of commending Jesus wherever they are. There could, however, be a better or worse decision in the light of loving God and others. Which option is the most loving for their fellow believers? If they were to go, would their church be discouraged and disheartened? Would their leaving communicate fear? Or is their presence actually making it harder for the local Christians? Perhaps leaving would help their brothers and sisters relate to, and reach out towards, those who oppose them? In any case, they must make this decision with their church. To decide on their own and then inform their church family, one way or the other, would not be loving towards them, and would not be an expression of the union they have with their brothers and sisters because of their union with Christ.

Six

Everyday in Christ

The Christian life can be frustrating. Things don't go the way we'd love them to go. People don't do the things we'd like them to do. We don't change the way we want to change. Relationships are messy, the church is full of sinners, and it often seems like everyone else is getting on better than we are. Sometimes discipleship seems like a long, hard road, and we'd love to just stop and rest a while – or find a faster vehicle to travel on!

In this final chapter, we will consider how our union with Christ really does reverberate into the most mundane, everyday parts of our lives.

In those moments of monotony or frustration our temptation is always to look to other things than Christ – to think we need something else as well as Christ:

a new kind of teaching; a new kind of power for living; a different set of relationships; a different church; some new techniques; a better list of rules to follow.

That's what the Christians in Colossae were in danger of doing. It is unclear whether the church at Colossae was under direct threat from false teaching, or whether Paul is addressing a potential heresy which might threaten the church in the future. Nor are the details of the heresy he addresses easy to define. Nevertheless, the big picture of the false teaching Paul is confronting seems to be this: Christ is sufficient in terms of entry into the Christian life, but to grow as Christians we need additional assistance. We need:

- the help of spiritual powers (1:16; 2:10,15,18)
- Old Testament laws, including circumcision (see 2:11-12,16-17)
- special knowledge and 'mysteries' (see 1:25-27; 2:2-4, 8, 18)
- self denial and abstinence (see 2:20-23)

Part of the problem in identifying the nature of the 'Colossian heresy' is that it seems to be a smorgasbord of ideas and convictions. Whoever the false teachers were and wherever they came from, they seem to have been particularly adept at choosing from a range of religions and influences.

Paul responds with a sublime presentation of the supremacy of Christ, both in terms of His person and work. Once we are 'in Him' we need nothing and no-one else: 'just as you received Christ Jesus as Lord, continue to live in him' (2:6, NIV). Elsewhere he writes:

- In Christ all the wisdom we need for godliness is ours (2:1-5)

- In Christ we have all the fullness of God (2:8-10)

- For all its attraction, religion in any of its forms can add nothing to Christ (2:20-23)

- We're united with Christ in His resurrection – set your sights on eternity (3:1-4)

- We're united with Christ in His death – put to death the old self (3:5-11)

Paul's central point is this: in Christ we have all we need for life and godliness.

We ought not to be surprised, however, at the danger the Colossian believers were in because of this false teaching. As we have seen, we are all prone to teaching that offers something more than we already have, or offers us an immediate solution to the problem of daily living. How many of us have not felt dissatisfied with our Christian life, or grown weary of the apparently endless struggle for godliness? There is nothing wrong with these feelings in and of themselves. They could actually be indicative of something altogether good. The danger is in where we go to deal with them. Do we go back to the gospel – back to Christ – or do we go somewhere else?

The sub-text of any heresy is always the same: it either distracts from the person of Christ, or detracts from the work of Christ. We need *more of* Christ, not *more than* Christ. Where do we find that? In the gospel. That is why Paul begins his letter to these vulnerable Christians by extolling the virtues of the gospel:

Of this you have heard before in the word of truth, the gospel, which has come to you, as indeed in the whole world it is bearing fruit and growing, as it also does among you, since the day you heard it and understood the grace of God in truth. (Col. 1:5-6)

The heart of the gospel is the truth concerning our union with Christ. Bob Dylan phrased it well when he wrote, 'You've done it all and there's no more anyone can pretend to do' in his haunting song, 'What Can I Do For You'. Again, the same point is made when we've considered the relationship between the indicatives and the imperatives of the gospel. The gospel calls us to be who we are 'in Christ', not somehow to work our way into Christ by our own efforts. The comprehensiveness of 1 Corinthians 1:30 is staggering and exhilarating: 'And because of him you are in Christ Jesus, who became to us wisdom from God, righteousness and sanctification and redemption'. But what does this look like in practice? How do these truths shape the lives of Christians in the mundane and the everyday?

1. *If we are united with Christ in His death, then die!*
In Mark 8, at a defining moment of His life and ministry, Jesus speaks clearly to the crowd about what it means to be His follower: 'If anyone would come after me, let him deny himself and take up his cross and follow me' (v. 34).

To those listening to that invitation, the words of Jesus would have meant just one thing – come and die: literally, physically and painfully. Following Jesus meant following Him all the way to the cross.

The context of this saying is a section built around the journey to Jerusalem (8:27–10:45). Mark has built this section on discipleship around three predictions by Jesus of His sufferings and death (8:31; 9:31; 10:33-34). So when James and John ask Jesus for positions of honour in His glory, Jesus responds by emphasising the necessity of suffering. And when the other ten become indignant, Jesus teaches them that leadership in the kingdom community is not to follow the pattern of the Gentiles, who lord it over those under them. Instead, it is to be based on the pattern of Jesus Himself: 'The Son of Man did not come to be served, but to serve, and to give his life as a ransom for many' (Mark 10:45).

Here we see a complex interaction between what Christ has done for us and what we do with Him. Although the two are distinct, they are nevertheless inseparable. Union with Christ means that Christ lived the life we could not live and died the death we should have died. But it means more than this: it also means that the life He lived is the life we live. Because we are in Him and share His Spirit, then the shape and manner of His life define the shape and manner of our life. Which means a life defined by the cross!

Self-denial is not a popular option for those of us who live in a materialistic, consumerist western culture. We define life by what we possess, which all too often is that which in fact possesses us. But the Christ who invites us to follow Him is the Christ Jesus who:

> ... being in very nature God, did not consider equality with God something to be used to his own advantage; rather, he made himself nothing by taking the very nature of a servant, being made in human likeness. And being found in appearance as a man, he humbled himself

by becoming obedient to death. Even death on a cross. (Phil. 2:6-8, NIV).

The wristbands with the letters WWJD written on them are a popular part of contemporary Christian culture, but the sentiment expressed by those letters has not met with universal approval. There is a sense in which it is more appropriate and effective to ask one another, 'What Did Jesus Do on the cross?' rather than speculate about What Would Jesus Do if He was in this situation. But we should not throw the proverbial baby out with the dirty bathwater. Because the life I live, I live in Him, then how He lived will define how I live.

Conformity to Christ, however, is not just a case of following His example, which is the primary weakness of the WWJD ethic. Calvin puts it like this: 'Our ingrafting signifies not only our conformity to the example of Christ, but also the secret union by which we grow together with him, in such a way that he revives us by his Spirit, and transfers his power to us.'[1] That power made available to us through our union with Him is, among other things, the power to say, 'No!' to ungodliness, to deny self and to die to the illusionary pleasure of sin.

Yes, it is much more than simply saying, 'No!' When we walk the way of the cross, we die to our old ambitions, we despise the criteria by which we previously assessed the good life and we loathe the woman or man we were. We see life in a radically new way. We see the way of the cross as being the good life: the life we were made to live. The cross is at the heart, not only of our redemption, but also of our everyday life. This works itself out in two ways.

1   John Calvin, *Commentaries*, Volume XXXVIII, Romans ch. 6, v. 5.

First, it works itself out in our experience of, and attitude towards, suffering and adversity. Calvin phrased it well when he wrote:

> How powerfully should it soften the bitterness of the cross, to think that the more we are afflicted with adversity, the surer we are made of our fellowship with Christ; by communion with whom our sufferings are not only blessed to us, but tend greatly to the furtherance of our salvation.[2]

Difficulties are an inevitable part of our life as Christians. Living in a fallen world means that the way of the cross is deeply counter-cultural. So much of life outside of Christ is one of difficulty-avoidance. We are willing to take any route, employ any measures and deploy any resources to ensure that we keep our suffering down to a minimum.

But in Christ many of those strategies are no longer an option. Living righteously in an unrighteous world puts us on an unavoidable collision course. As it was for Jesus, so it is for us. If Christ's whole life was 'a sort of perpetual cross',[3] then we who are united with Him can expect nothing less. Such suffering is a real participation in the sufferings of Christ. This is what Calvin described as 'a great consolation',[4] because if we share in His death, we will also, by God's grace, share in His life and glory. Through our afflictions 'our fellowship with Christ is confirmed'.[5]

Second, it works itself out in our attitude towards ourselves and others. There was a time when, in Adam, like Adam, I wanted to define for myself what was good and

---

2   John Calvin, *Institutes*, 3.8.1.

3   Ibid.

4   John Calvin, *Commentaries*, Volume XLII, Philippians ch. 3, v. 10.

5   John Calvin, *Institutes*, 3.8.1.

evil. Good was that which brought me happiness without reference to anything else or regard for anyone else. Evil was that which in any way deprived me of that happiness. I viewed the world as my world, and imagined myself as god. But now I am in Christ, and like Christ, I take up the cross and walk as He walked. I no longer walk where my father Adam walked.

In Christ, the way of the cross is the way of service because in Christ I am a servant. It is not simply something I do: it is someone I am. The heart that desired self-promotion arising out of self-obsession is radically renewed. Being made in the image of God means we are lovers because the God whose image we bear is, in His Trinitarian life, a lover. But in Adam, sin reorientated my heart so that God-centred, other-focused love was replaced with self-centred, self-focused love. In Christ, the image of the invisible God (cf. Col. 1:15), we are restored to that image and become the lovers we were made to be: lovers of God and lovers of others. This now shapes the everyday life we live. We no longer live for ourselves. We display God's image and glory as, out of love for Him, we love others and intentionally pursue their good.

2.   If we are united with Christ in His resurrection, then live!
We should be aware of what has been described as the 'now-and-not-yet' tension of the Christian life. We should also be careful to avoid the trap of an over-realised eschatology. But in reaction, many Christians become prone to an under-realised eschatology and adopt a loser's ethic as though failure is not only normal but virtuous.

As we have affirmed consistently, through our union with Christ we participate in the life and glory of Christ's resurrection, which is a pledge of our resurrection. We also share in His ascension into glory:

> Christ did not ascend to heaven privately for himself, to dwell there alone, but rather that it might be the common inheritance of all the godly, and that in this way the head might be united to the members.[6]

The flow of Paul's argument in Colossians 3:1-5 is instructive:

> Since, then, you have been raised with Christ, set your hearts on things above, where Christ is, seated at the right hand of God. Set your minds on things above, not on earthly things. For you died, and your life is now hidden with Christ in God. When Christ, who is your life, appears, then you also will appear with him in glory. Put to death, therefore ... (NIV)

This reflects the 'now-and-not-yet' tension. Our resurrection life is now hidden; and yet it remains the point of reference for Paul's call to comprehensive godliness. In Christ we have risen to newness of life, and the call to godliness is to walk in that newness of life.

Our lives as individual believers and our shared life as His people are to be lived in such a way that they give a glimpse and offer a foretaste of the life that is to come. We live the resurrection life that is ours in Christ through the power of the Spirit. We do that as we say an emphatic 'No!' to sin and a resounding 'Yes!' to godliness. We do that as we serve others. We do that as we learn contentment in any and every circumstance. We do that as we rejoice in our suffering. Look at Philippians 3:10:

---

6   John Calvin, Commentaries, Volume XXXV, John chapter 14, verse 2.

> I want to know Christ—yes, to know the power of his resurrection and participation in his sufferings, becoming like him in his death, and so, somehow, attaining to the resurrection from the dead. (NIV)

In respect to the phrase 'participation in his sufferings', Marcus Bockmuehl makes this helpful comment: 'To participate in Christ's sufferings was for Paul ... a way of relating the constant, and in his view eschatological, experience of affliction and tribulation to Christ.'[7]

But here is the question: why does resurrection come before sufferings, when temporally and logically it seems to make more sense for the order to be reversed? For this reason: because the power of Christ's resurrection life in us is the power to suffer. In Christ we have strength not to live lives of uninterrupted self-fulfilment, but rather to lay down our lives for the gospel. The Christian life can be a long, hard slog. It does involve suffering and mistreatment. Our union with Christ empowers us precisely for those times in which we are overlooked, maligned, mistreated and misunderstood; it gives us strength to keep laying down our lives in those moments when we wonder if it really is worth carrying on. Indeed, our resurrection life shines brightest in how we suffer.

We will conclude by looking at two particular areas of everyday life in order to see how our union with Christ flows out into the most mundane of everyday experiences.

Everyday Prayer

Prayer is the succulent fruit of our union with Christ. In Christ we are adopted children of God, enjoying all the

---

7   Markus Bockmuehl, *The Epistle to the Philippians* (Continuum, 2006), p. 215.

benefits of sonship along with our Elder Brother. In Him, we not only enjoy unfettered access into the presence of God, but we actually inhabit that hallowed space. Prayer does not bring us into the presence of God; we pray because, in Christ, we are always in the presence of God. In Christ our conscience is clear because the debt is paid. The Father only ever smiles upon us, and because we are in Christ, He delights to hear us pray. He welcomes us with open arms and lifts us on to His knee so we might pour out our heart to Him.

Union with Christ lifts prayer from the realm of religion and places it firmly in the domain of an intimate relationship. This is why there is no procedure, no preparation and no pre-determined time or season. In Christ, prayer is an everyday, moment-by-moment relational privilege. Yes, prayer is an expression of our need, and it does reveal our sense of dependency. But, first and foremost, prayer is what we do because of who we are in Christ.

Christians are those in Christ, and those in Christ pray. It really is as simple as that. How we pray is a matter of personal preference. We may have a pattern of formal prayer: a routine for when we pray specifically and in an uninterrupted way. So-called 'Quiet Times' can be exceptionally beneficial, and even advisable. But our prayer should neither be confined to, nor defined by, those times, any more than a marriage should be confined to, or defined by, a so-called 'date night'.

So pray when you're joyful. Pray when you are sad. Pray when you are victorious. Pray when you are defeated. Pray when you witness for Christ. Pray when you run away scared. Just pray. Because this is what our union with Christ means.

Imagine these two very different scenarios.

Scenario 1

Your day begins well with prayer and bible study, before a leisurely breakfast. On your drive to work you have the opportunity to show remarkable grace to two rude and aggressive drivers by letting them into the queue with a smile. Once at the office you work diligently, and take the opportunity afforded by coffee and lunch to speak to your co-workers about Jesus. The afternoon passes uneventfully, allowing you to get home in good time to help your kids finish their homework, so you can all go out to the home group BBQ. Whilst there, you get to share the gospel with some neighbours, one of whom makes what seems to be a genuine profession of faith. You go home rejoicing, put your kids to bed with a prayer and a smile, before settling down with your spouse and your Daily Devotional to end the day giving thanks to God.

Scenario 2

Your day begins with you sleeping through your alarm. When you do wake up you are already five minutes late for work. Having no time for breakfast, you jump in your car hoping to make up lost time, only to find your way blocked by a very long tail-back. You cannot believe the number of idiots that have chosen today of all days to drive, and you make it clear to them just what you think of them. When you finally get to work, you shout at one of your colleagues and when asked a direct question about your faith, you mumble incoherently into your coffee cup and turn to the advertising pages of the newspaper. You leave early to beat the traffic only to find out that the idiots you encountered on the way in have all decided to do the same – and brought their friends along as well. You want to go to the home group BBQ but the kids are all in a foul mood and you end up sending them to bed early. Your spouse is annoyed by your reaction to them, resulting in a big argument. As you both sit there in bed, you glance at your Daily Devotional, but for some reason the prospect of reading it and praying together is the last thing on your mind.

Honesty requires all of us to admit that our response to Scenario 1 is more likely to include prayer than it would Scenario 2. In Scenario 2 prayer would seem presumptuous and hypocritical. But the wonderful truth is this: union with Christ means that prayer is as permissible and desirable in Scenario 2 as it is in Scenario 1. Union with Christ means the Father will be as delighted when we pray in both scenarios. The first scenario does not make our prayer more acceptable or our praying more desirable. The second scenario does not make it less so. Union with Christ means prayer should be our response in both situations. Sin does not make God less disposed towards us for the simple reason that we are accepted, not in and of ourselves, but in the beloved Son whose person and work are more than sufficient to cover all our sin. When the Father looks on us, He sees His Son and is always nothing less than '*well pleased*'. Because we are 'in Christ', the call of the gospel is always 'Come!' and it is always 'Pray!' Of course, that is not what Satan wants us to think. He wants us to wallow in our failure and compound it with unbelieving prayerlessness. But we are in Christ, so what does it matter what he says? He cannot reach us there; he has no right of access.

EVERYDAY MARRIAGE

We have already seen that the marriage covenant between a man and a woman points to the beautiful intimacy of the relationship between Christ and His church. Marriage is not, in the first instance, for the sake of marriage. It points beyond itself to something greater and infinitely richer, namely the staggering reality of God's love for His people. This being the case, we can see how union with Christ impacts the shape of our relationships with one another, and particularly the relationship between a husband and wife.

In Colossians 3, Paul's motivation for unity is the new life which we have put on *in Christ* (vv. 9-11). The sins Paul highlights all lead to discord and division, whereas the specific behaviours and attitudes of love which he promotes – compassion, kindness, humility, gentleness, patience, bearing with one another, forgiveness, love which binds together in perfect unity (vv. 13-14) – all point to, and express the unity that is ours in Christ. As he puts it succinctly, we are members of one body. This is the same unity which primarily unites husband and wife. Union in marriage does not spring in the first instance from the sexual act. That physical union is as close as it is possible for any two people to get, and it is an important aspect of a godly marriage. But if we look to sex as the primary determination of unity in marriage we are giving it too much significance. Full union in marriage is only possible when husband and wife are both united to Christ. Because of *that* union they are truly united with one another. And that communion of believers, which springs from union with Christ, is something that all believers enjoy regardless of marital status.

First, this is good news for those who are single. In contemporary Christian culture we tend to elevate marriage as the inevitable and most desirable end of adolescence. Young girls make lists of the attributes they desire in a husband and pray that God would bring such a godly young man into their lives. Young men scan the single girls in their church. If not consciously, we subconsciously communicate that fulfilment, discipleship and godly service in adulthood are bound up in finding a marriage partner. But the doctrine of union with Christ shows the idolatry of this thinking. Union with Christ means that genuine and meaningful fellowship with one another is part and parcel of life in Christ's body. This is not to denigrate marriage in any way. Marriage is the most intimate of all human relationships, and as such plays a unique role. But human marriage is not the 'be-all-and-end-all'. It is not the relational destination point for everyone. Contrary to popular opinion, singleness is not being 'left on the shelf': it is being purchased by the Lord for another purpose that he, as the owner, has in mind.

Second, this is also good news for those who are married. Because being 'in Christ' is our defining identity, being married isn't. Once I appreciate that, then I can enjoy marriage for what it is, rather than for what I imagine I need it to be. Out of a deep sense and thankfulness for being 'in Christ', the husband is free to be the husband he is called to be. He is no longer enslaved by his marriage, or by the need to be seen to have a successful marriage, or by his wife's happiness at the expense of her holiness. By revelling in her union with Christ, the wife is also liberated to be the helper the Lord calls her to be. She no longer need fear her husband, crave his approval or be intimidated by his demands or expectations.

Third, this is good news for those whose marriages are falling apart, or have fallen apart. The sad reality of life in a fallen world is that marriages fail. No one goes into a marriage thinking they will become one of those statistics, but sadly it will happen to some. Contrary to popular opinion, however, not all failed marriages are 'six of one and half a dozen of the other'. It is possible to be a faithful, loving, godly wife and for your husband to walk slowly away from the Lord and you. Without knowing who you are 'in Christ', you will not be able to bear the failure or endure the pain of that breakdown. Being 'in Christ' does not mean any of us are immune from gut-wrenching pain and heart-breaking disappointment. It does not mean we will have any more insight into why the Lord does what He does in the way that He does it. But it does mean we know where our treasure lies. It does mean we know who we are. It does mean we can rest, knowing that for all of the inscrutability of His ways, the Lord is good, His purposes certain and we are secure.

PORTERBROOK NETWORK

Is all about biblical training for mission and ministry, where you are, through our book series' and two curriculums:

 - Porterbrook Learning
 - Porterbrook Seminary

PORTERBROOK LEARNING

Porterbrook Learning is an online training curriculum, for equipping Christians for ministry in the local church and church planting. It connects the heart and mission to the Bible story.

24 online modules to choose from covering:

 - Bible and Doctrine
 - Character
 - Church
 - World

PORTERBROOK SEMINARY

Porterbrook Seminary allows you to study in-depth in the context of your ministry over 3 years. Get input from world-class theologians and pastor-practitioners that will shape your ministry.

 - For leaders and planters to train in the context of ministry
 - An affordable and flexible college level course that prepares people for leadership in local church ministries
 - 3 years (or study a year at a time), 10 hours study a week, 3 residentials and 7 assignments a year

For more information visit www.Porterbrooknetwork.org

Also available in this series...

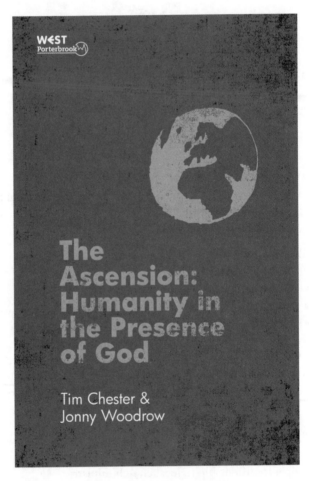

ISBN 978-1-78191-144-0

The Ascension

Humanity in the Presence of God

TIM CHESTER AND JONNY WOODROW

Who is this ascended Jesus? He is King, Priest and man and is still at work. Ultimately He is humanity in the presence of God. Here we discover how we are a part of the Ascension. With the Spirit's enlightening we can begin to understand the Ascension. Tim Chester introduces us to this important doctrine.

> Chester and Woodrow have given us a gift that will lift our eyes from this temporal horizon to the steppes of eternal joys of our High Priest in heaven.
>
> Eric C. Redmond
>
> Executive Pastoral Assistant and Bible Professor in Residence New Canaan Baptist Church, Washington, DC; Council Member, The Gospel Coalition

> The writers show us the Bible's answers to these questions and many more. If you have ever wondered why the ascension is critical to being a disciple of Jesus or why it wasn't just a bad strategy by God that removed the main evidence for Christianity, you will find plenty of help here.
>
> Marcus Honeysett
>
> Director of Living Leadership and author of *Finding Joy*, Kent, England

Tim Chester is an author, Pastor of The Crowded House, Sheffield and Director of Porterbrook Seminary. He is married with two daughters.

Jonny Woodrow is the Director of Porterbrook Network and Pastor of The Crowded House, Loughborough. He is married with four children.

Christian Focus Publications

Our mission statement –

STAYING FAITHFUL

In dependence upon God we seek to impact the world through literature faithful to His infallible Word, the Bible. Our aim is to ensure that the Lord Jesus Christ is presented as the only hope to obtain forgiveness of sin, live a useful life and look forward to heaven with Him.

Our Books are published in four imprints:

CHRISTIAN FOCUS

Popular works including biographies, commentaries, basic doctrine and Christian living.

CHRISTIAN HERITAGE

Books representing some of the best material from the rich heritage of the church.

MENTOR

Books written at a level suitable for Bible College and seminary students, pastors, and other serious readers. The imprint includes commentaries, doctrinal studies, examination of current issues and church history.

CF4•K

Children's books for quality Bible teaching and for all age groups: Sunday school curriculum, puzzle and activity books; personal and family devotional titles, biographies and inspirational stories – Because you are never too young to know Jesus!

Christian Focus Publications Ltd,
Geanies House, Fearn, Ross-shire,
IV20 1TW, Scotland, United Kingdom.
www.christianfocus.com